Just Add Water

Just Add Water

Barbara G. Salsbury

INTERNATIONAL STANDARD BOOK NUMBER
0-88290-011-0

Thirty-sixth Printing, January 1981

Printed and Distributed in the
United States of America
by
Horizon
Publishers &
Distributors

———————

P.O. Box 490
50 South 500 West
Bountiful, Utah 84010

TABLE OF CONTENTS

TABLE OF CHARTS

ABOUT THE AUTHOR

Barbara G. Salsbury

Many years of experimentation and study concerning the varied uses of dehydrated foods have made Barbara G. Salsbury well qualified to write **Just Add Water.** For more than fifteen years she has been actively involved in testing and developing her own recipes and food storage program. She has become a well known lecturer on the subject and has spoken to many groups throughout California. She has developed most of the recipes in this book, as well as a emergency situation program for families.

Mrs. Salsbury spent her childhood in Ohio and California. She attended El Camino Junior College in California.

The author is a childhood convert to The Church of Jesus Christ of Latter-day Saints, and has been active in a variety of Church responsibilities. She has been a teacher of adult women in the Relief Society program and a leader of young children in the Primary organization. Her love of music and dance have kept her closely involved with choir and youth organizations. She is recipient of the Golden Gleaner award from the Young Womens Mutual Improvement Association, the Mormon Church's youth program. She is an author of poetry and plays which have been used in various Church programs. Because of her preparedness in the food storage and usage areas, she has been a frequent speaker at Fireside programs and Relief Society demonstrations. Her husband Larry is a Latter-day Saint Bishop. They are the parents of a son and daughter.

HORIZON PUBLISHERS is pleased to publish **Just Add Water,** by Barbara G. Salsbury. We wish her continuing success in her future endeavors!

CHAPTER I

DEHYDRATED FOODS

Differences Between "Dehydrated" and "Dried" Foods

You and I have been using dehydrated foods and products for a long time. They are called "convenience foods." Gelatins, gravy mixes, salad dressings, cake mixes, soup mixes, onions, non-fat milk, instant cream, instant potatoes, and any instant or prepared mix are all dehydrated food products. These foods are very good when properly prepared. A wise homemaker should plan to use dehydrated items in her meal preparation.

There is a difference between dehydrated foods and the dried foods which are purchased in the supermarket. With dried foods the water is evaporated leaving a moisture content of approximatly 25%. This allows the product to remain soft and pliable. These items, such as figs, raisins and prunes will store 12 - 18 months in proper conditions. Dehydrated fruits and vegetables are processed under a high vacuum and a very low drying temperature. This processing makes it possible to remove practically all of the water. The moisture content is reduced to 2% - 3%. The product becomes shriveled and very brittle.

Dehydrated foods retain their vitamin value because it has not been cooked out in the canning process.

Both types of processed fruit are dusted with a weak solution of sulphide to retain the natural color. This solution can be rinsed off, or will cook off, without any effect to the taste of the food.

Dehydrated Food More Economical than Canned Food

How does the cost of dehydrated food compare with the same canned product? Dehydrated foods will often allow your food budget to go at least twice as far. Even when compared with home canned products, dehydrated foods are economical. This is especially true during the winter months when most fresh produce is out of season and the prices soar.

One case No. 303 cans equals 24 cans. One case of wet pack product would cost approximately the same as one No. 10 can of the same item in dehydrated form. With the dehydrated products you do not pay for the water, peelings, or pits, just the product without any waste.

For example, suppose you've allotted $5.00 for your storage budget this month to buy fruit cocktail. The supermarket has brand X, No. 303 can on sale at 5/$1.00. This is a very good price. You bring home 25 cans. When drained and measured the amount of fruit per can is approximately 1 cup. This will give you 25 cups.

In contrast, one No. 10 can of dehydrated fruit galaxy weighs 44 ounces. One cup equals 4 ounces dry weight. One can contains 11 cups dry. However, when the water is returned to the product, there will be approximately 33 cups of fruit.

Chart 1

Dehydrated Goods Compared with Canned Foods

Canned Item	Can Size	Weight	Amount of Liquid	Amount of Product
Fruit Cocktail	No. 303	17 oz.	1 cup	1 cup
Green Beans	No. 303	16 oz.	1 cup	2 cups
Peach halves	No. 303	17 oz.	1 cup	1 cup
Peach slices	No. 303	17 oz.	1 cup	1¼ cup
Peas	No. 303	17 oz.	1¾ cup	¾ cup

The above items are the wet pack cans you buy from the market shelves. In most cases half or more of the weight of the can is water.

Dehydrated Item	Dry Amount	Weight	Water Added	Yield
Fruit Galaxy	1 cup	4 oz.	1½ cups	2½ cups
Green Beans	1 cup	2 oz.	1¼ cups	2½ cups
Peaches, sliced	1 cup	4 oz.	1¼ cups	2 cups
Peas	1 cup	4 oz.	2 cups	2 1/3 cups

Two cups of water were added to each of the dehydrated products above. After 24 hours the excess liquid was poured off and measured. This was done in order to arrive at the amount of yield.

The results of the comparison are obvious. Dehydrated foods have approximately double the yield of canned foods, even though their cost is much lower.

Lower Weight and Easier Storage of Dehydrated Foods

One case of canned food weighs approximately 24 pounds. The same item of dehydrated food would weigh from 36 to 45 ounces, or one No. 10 can.

A complete storeroom is often needed for canned goods. The space required for a family of five, including wheat, grains, and milk, is approximately 5' x 8' and 6' - 7' high. If the occasion arose and you had to move, it would be hard (some have said impossible) to move a year's supply of wet pack products. We've had one year's supply of dehydrated foods and grains in our station wagon at one time.

Most commonly used foods are now available in dehydrated form. A partial list includes:

Chart 2

Commonly Available Dehydrated Foods

Apples: nuggets, sliced
Apricots: sliced
Banana: flakes, sliced
Date Nuggets
Fruit Galaxy (comparable to
* fruit cocktail)*
Peaches: sliced
Pears
Prunes
Cheese
Eggs
Milk
Beans: green
Beets: diced
Carrots: sliced, diced
Celery: sliced
Corn
Onions: sliced, chopped, diced
Peas
Peppers: green & red, diced

Potatoes: sliced, flakes, diced,
* shredded*
Soup Blend
Spinach
Stew Mix
Tomato Crystals (used   in
* cooking: to make juice*
* sauce, paste, soups)*
Yams
Multi-purpose Food (basically
* used as an extender*
Meat Substitutes (different
* companies use   different*
* names for the same type*
* of product)*
* Bacon Bits*
* Beef*
* Burger Granules*
* Chicken*
* Ham*
* Meat Loaf Mix*

Packaging of Dehydrated Foods

Dehydrated products are available in various sized containers. Most companies manufacturing and selling these foods have basically the same sizes available. Dehydrated foods are usually packaged in one or more of the following styles:

(1) **Pantry Pak:** A small cellophane or plastic bag. This usually contains 5-10 servings. This is a good trial size to work with. If you desire to try a certain item before purchasing a large amount, this would be the size package to use. The Pantry Pak is the size most individuals take camping.

(2) **Hostess:** A cellophane or plastic bag. Usually this size bag contains the same amount as would a No. 10 can of the same item. Perhaps if you already had an empty can, or would be using

it immediately, this size would be the one to buy. Like the Pantry Pak, this would not store on a shelf indefinitely.

(3)   **No. 2½ Can:** This can is about the size of the one-pound shortening can. The dry weight of the contents, and reconstituted weight will vary with each product.

(4)   **No. 10 Can:** This can is the size of a one-gallon paint can. The dry weight and reconstituted weight of the contents will vary with each product. This is the most popular size container when purchasing dehydrated fruits and vegetables for storage. It is a workable size for most individuals or families. It is also a good shelf size.

(5)   **5 Gallon Can:** You can purchase some items in this size can. You may also find a source for these cans close to home and put items in cans yourself, such as wheat, milk, flour, macaroni, beans, and rice. Make sure that the can purchased has the type lid that will seal. The items that you put in your own cans represents a money savings. However, you must remember these are not vacuum sealed so they are not a "store and forget" item.

(6)   **Bulk:** Some companies offer the dehydrated items bulk in bags. For large families and economical planning, this is a very practical way to obtain your food. It requires a little more work and effort on your part, as you must find containers to put these items in. Purchasing food in this form is worthwhile at times because it allows you to use your budget to the fullest extent.

Storage Life of Dehydrated Foods

Many dehydrated products are prepared in vacuum-sealed cans and have a reasonable long shelf life if left unopened. Most will keep from five to ten years. Dry milk, eggs, or any product with milk or eggs in it, have a shorter shelf life.

How long will a dehydrated item keep after it has been opened? With a tight-fitting plastic lid on top, it will keep as long as is required to use it. If it takes several months to use an item, the product will become softer than when it was first opened, because every time the lid is removed it absorbs moisture. This will not change the flavor, however, nor alter the food value.

In comparison, most wet pack products can be kept for only two to five years, depending upon the food. However, you have little way of knowing how long the product has been canned and stored before you buy it. Perhaps the sale fruit cocktail is already two years old when you buy it. A consistent plan of rotation must be worked out to use a canned food storage plan effectively.

Chart 3

Approximate Shelf Life for Typical Dehydrated Foods and Related Items
(If product is in vacuum-sealed cans)

Items	Years	Items	Years
Baking Powder & Soda	5-10	Sugar, white	Indefinite
Barley	10 plus	Tomato Crystals, DH	10 plus
Cornstarch	5-10	Wheat, whole kernel	Indefinite
Flour, white	2	Yeast, dry	2 plus
Flour, wheat	2	Boullion, cube	3-5
Honey	Indefinite	Boullion, granule	5
Milk, instant, non-fat	2	Gelatin, unflavored	Indefinite
Milk, regular, non-fat	2	Gelatin, dessert	10 plus
Multi-purpose food	Indefinite	Macaroni products	5
Onions, DH	10 plus	Soup Blend, DH	10 plus
Peppers, green DH	10 plus	Stew Blend, DH	10 plus
Potatoes, DH	10 plus	Meat Substitutes	2-3
Rice, brown	2	Spices	2-3
Rice, white	10 plus	Vegetables, DH	10 plus
Salad Blend, DH	10 plus	Beans & Peas, dried	10 plus
Salt	Indefinite	Eggs, whole, DH	2-5
Shortening	5 plus	Fruit, DH	10 plus

Taste and Texture of Dehydrated Foods

During the dehydration process foods become very small, shriveled, and hard. This does not alter their taste at all. When prepared properly, these foods are very tasty. However, some individuals may feel that they would have to get used to them. It would be wise, perhaps to buy in small quantities, until you are certain which foods will be the family favorites.

One important thing to remember in planning your food purchases and storage items: Do *not* buy anything that your family does not like or will not eat! The only exception might be an item that could be used for medicinal purposes, such as prunes.

CHAPTER II

HOW TO PLAN A STORAGE PROGRAM

The Goal: A Balanced Supply for a Year

In this day of uncertainty and unrest, it is a wise plan for a family to be prepared for any emergency by having a good supply of food on hand. Who knows when natural disasters, unemployment, or even the ravages of riots or war may strike? The time may come when the foresight of having a good supply of food on hand may mean the prevention of much discomfort and distress to your family.

A goal which many families have sought to achieve has been to have a year's supply of food, in balanced and appropriate varieties, on hand at all times. We recommend this goal as a worthwhile endeavor and suggest you make it your objective.

We all work on strict budgets. We don't usually have an excess amount of money waiting until we can find a use for it. Many of us have tried to build our storage program by purchasing the "buy of the month"—cheese, milk, a can of eggs, canned goods on sale. At the end of the year we have twelve different items (if we haven't used some in the meantime). This approach has proved a dismal failure for most of the families who have attempted it.

A New Approach

Let us suggest a new approach! First, you need to take the time to inventory *exactly* what foods and supplies you already have in your cupboards and shelves. Don't fudge and don't cheat, not even a little! Write it all down! If you've been feeding a family for any length of time, it will surprise you how much you really have placed here and there. From what you have on hand, start to plan your menus, to use what you have. It might mean eating homemade soup every night for a week, and oatmeal every morning for breakfast, but it allows you to utilize your regular food budget money to purchase food storage items.

Your first two or three or four orders of storage foods should be purchased immediately so that you don't have to purchase groceries. The items purchased first should balance out and extend these foods which you have inventoried. For example, if you have on hand some tuna, noodles and other items for main dishes, then you may want to obtain a can of dehydrated vegetables and a can of dehydrated fruit. Keep in mind that at all times your food should be planned and balanced, so that if some emergency should arise you would be able to prepare balanced meals. It would not be wise to purchase all of your fruit first, nor all of your vegetables, nor all of the meat substitutes.

Upon obtaining your dehydrated foods, work them into your every day meals. If you would purchase even one can of fruit, one can of vegetables, a meat product, some eggs, and milk, you would be able to have a variety of good meals.

Now you should habitually order! Every grocery shopping day —think *dehydrated!* Eventually, work more and more percentage of your grocery budget money into storage and include dehydrated foods in *all* of your meals.

This plan serves two very important purposes! It allows you the *financial means* with which to purchase your storage. Every two weeks or every month, religiously, systematically, order and use. Once you have enough variety from which to make your every day meals, you build your supply until you obtain your goal. Second, it gives you *experience.* You learn how to measure, season, cook, and serve all of these products. Don't get discouraged! It all takes time, but this time and experience are priceless. Documented studies show, over and over again, that a time of emergency is no time to be trying new experiments with food. In some places people, especially children, will starve rather than be force fed a "new" diet. In troubled times, if the body has not become accustomed to eating what you have stored, this could bring you more havoc than help. Your family could become extremely sick if suddenly they were taken from the "luxury" foods, lacking roughage and vitamins, and put on a 100% wheat diet. This could bring on painful constipation or diarrhea. It is only fair to ourselves and our families, that we get them used to eating other foods now. Laugh together, then try again, while you still have an opportunity to learn and try. It is important to develop your family's taste for the foods you store, now.

Importance of Proper Attitude

Your *attitude* is all important! If you involve your family and are happy at the prospect of eating dehydrated foods, you most likely will succeed. If you are doubtful and say, "Well, I guess we'll have to eat this stuff now," you've already lost.

This food is good, healthful, extremely economical, and is a way to fulfill a commandment of our Heavenly Father. It is with this thought in mind that I have tried to combine and put together a few of the things I have gleaned from my years of studying and practicing food storage. If you can just catch the spirit of it, with a few thoughts and ideas, then it has all been worthwhile.

Planning with the Weekly Food Chart

You and your family are individuals with likes and dislikes. You cannot be expected to store exactly what another family would store. You must arrive at your own storage plan, as to what items you wish to store. Perhaps a way to begin to figure how much you need would be to use the accompanying "Weekly Food Chart." If you will copy this chart and tape it on the front of your refrigerator door, it will prove to be useful. *Everytime* anything is used in cooking or for eating, MARK IT DOWN. Faithfully keep track of the items your family eats for one week, two, or three. This will allow you to calculate very closely the amount of food your family eats under normal conditions. It will enable you to see at a glance the different kinds of food your family uses the most. This information will be very important and useful in the proper planning of a storage program. It could easily be extended to a one-year plan.

Two Suggested Storage Plan Using Dehydrated Foods

To aid you in planning your storage program, two sample plans are presented here. Quantities are shown for from one to ten adults for one year in each plan. The first plan uses many fruits and vegetables and minimizes the use of sugar and milk.

Chart 4

WEEKLY FOOD CHART

AMOUNTS USED

ITEMS	SUNDAY	MONDAY	TUESDAY	WEDNESDAY	THURSDAY	FRIDAY	SATURDAY
Milk-Cheese							
Eggs-Butter							
Bread							
Cereal							
Vegetables							
Fruit							
Meat							
Flour-Sugar							
Condiments							
Other							

Chart 5

A Suggested Food Storage Plan Using Dehydrated Foods—No. 1

Item	Number in Family									
	1	2	3	4	5	6	7	8	9	10
Vegetables—No. 10 can	5	10	15	20	25	30	35	40	45	50
Juice Crystals—lbs.	12	24	36	48	60	72	84	96	108	120
Potatoes—No. 10 can	8	16	24	32	40	48	56	64	72	80
Fruit—No. 10 can	8	16	24	32	40	48	56	64	72	80
Rice—No. 10 can	8	16	24	32	40	48	56	64	72	80
Milk—quarts	150	300	450	600	750	900	1050	1200	1350	1500
Multi-purpose Food—No. 10 can	8	16	24	32	40	48	56	64	72	80
Beans, dry—No. 10 can	2	4	6	8	10	12	14	16	18	20
Eggs—1-lb can	3	6	9	12	15	18	21	24	27	30
Gelatin—1-lb can	1	2	3	4	5	6	7	8	9	10
Boullion—1-lb can	2	4	6	8	10	12	14	16	18	20
Canned meat	25	50	75	100	125	150	175	200	225	250
Wheat—5 gal. can	4	8	12	16	20	24	28	32	36	40
Cereal—No. 10 can	1	2	3	4	5	6	7	8	9	10
Macaroni—No. 10 can	1	2	3	4	5	6	7	8	9	10
Cornmeal—No. 10 can	1	2	3	4	5	6	7	8	9	10
Yeast—2½ lb. can	1	2	3	4	5	6	7	8	9	10
Sugar or honey—lbs.	25	50	75	100	125	150	175	200	225	250
Salt—lbs.	5	10	15	20	25	30	35	40	45	50

The second plan is better balanced.

Chart 6

A Suggested Food Storage Plan Using Dehydrated Foods—No. 2

Item	Number in Family									
	1	2	3	4	5	6	7	8	9	10
Wheat—5-gal. cans	5	10	15	20	25	30	35	40	45	50
Milk—quarts	365	730	1095	1460	1825	2190	2555	2920	3185	3650
Gelatin—24-oz. cans	4	8	12	16	20	24	28	32	36	40
Eggs—1-lb. cans	3	6	9	12	15	18	21	24	27	30
Boullion—1-lb cans	2	4	6	8	10	12	14	16	18	20
Cereal—No. 10 can	4	8	12	16	20	24	28	32	36	40
Peas—No. 10 can	5	10	15	20	25	30	35	40	45	50
Beans—No. 10 can	5	10	15	20	25	30	35	40	45	50
Rice—No. 10 can	5	10	15	20	25	30	35	40	45	50
Potatoes—No. 10 can	4	8	12	16	20	24	28	32	36	40
Vegetables—No. 10 can	4	8	12	16	20	24	28	32	36	40
Stew—No. 10 can	4	8	12	16	20	24	28	32	36	40
Onions—No. 10 can	2	4	6	8	10	12	14	16	18	20
Tomato crystals—No. 10 can	2	4	6	8	10	12	14	16	18	20
Fruit—No. 10 can	5-6	10	15	20	25	30	35	40	45	50
Juice crystals—24 oz.	4	8	12	16	20	24	28	32	36	40
Sugar or honey—lbs.	60	120	180	240	300	360	420	480	540	600
Salt—lbs.	5	10	15	20	25	30	35	40	45	50

Estimating Annual Needs

You will need to determine how much each member of your family will eat in a year's time if you are going to reach your food storage and family preparedness goal. A basis for comparison of your calculations can be found on the following chart, which is based on figures furnished by the Utah Department of Health (1956). One adult will eat approximately the following in one year:

Chart 7

Average Annual Food Consumption

Milk	365 qts.
Eggs	30 doz.
Meat	150 lbs.
Green & Yellow Vegetables	150 lbs.
Potatoes	150 lbs.
Citrus & Tomato fruits	120 lbs.
Apples	75 lbs.
Other Fruits & Vegetables	200 lbs.
Flour, Cereals, Breads	200 lbs.
(Count ½ lb. of bread as 1 lb. of flour)	
Dried Beans, Peas, Nuts	15 lbs.
Fats & Oils	65 lbs.
(butter, cream, shortening, bacon, salad oils)	
Syrup, Sugar, Preserves, Honey, etc.	60 lbs.

Amounts will vary according to usage and appetite in various families, naturally.

Running Inventory

An easy way to keep track of what you store is to set up a "running inventory" in a looseleaf notebook. Every time you add or take away from your stock it can be quickly recorded, and you are able to see at a glance how close to your goal you really are. Should it be necessary to start using those storage items you have replaced, you would be able to tell immediately how long your stores will last. You can also determine what kind of menus can be planned from them. For example:

Chart 8

Running Inventory Example

Item	Total Amount Needed Annually	Amount on Hand	Amount to Obtain
Peaches	7-No. 10	4 5	3 2
Potatoes	10-No. 10	2	8
Corn	6-No. 10	0 3	6 3
Apple Slices	6-No. 10	6	0
Wheat	10-5 gal.	4	6

Storing Water

Dehydrated food storage requires the storage of some water. It would be practically impossible to store a year's supply of water, but we should store some! The amount of water we store, just like the rest of our storage, will be strictly an individual thing.

In planning your supply, don't short change your children. Count every individual as an adult. You don't know when the need to use storage items will arise. When I planned our storage my boy was three. He didn't eat very much then. You can imagine the difference now that he is eleven. I wouldn't have been fair if I had considered him in terms of having a baby appetite.

In some areas five-gallon plastic bottles with an interchangeable spigot are now available. You may prefer to store water in them. Canned water may also be purchased.

The *Civil Defense Manual* suggest seven gallons for each individual as a *minimum* emergency supply. This would barely be enough for drinking and limited cooking, not allowing any for bathing or washing.

If something should happen locally to temporarily sever the water supply, water can be drawn from the water heater and water closets. These contain enough water to help in an emergency situation.

To store water successfully in plastic bleach jugs, rinse them out carefully and put two drops of bleach per quart into each bottle. (Make sure the lids are clean.) To store water in glass jars, prepare them by placing them in boiling water. Boil pint jars for 20 minutes, quart jars for 25 minutes, and gallon jars for 30 minutes.

If store water tastes flat, it probably lacks air. Simply pour the water from one container into another three or four times to freshen it.

Make your storage program a habit. Keep one thought foremost in mind. YOU can do it! It can be done! Allow your thoughts to become so geared to it that every paper you pick up, every sale you see, all remind you of your goal. Soon you will obtain it, and with it the peace of mind that comes from knowing you are prepared for any emergency that may arise.

Storage of Non-Food Items

Other things besides food should be included in a storage program. Many such items are in your home already. Store those things which you would actually need to maintain your home if you had no way to purchase them. You can take advantage of current sales. Some of the items considered necessities have a short shelf life. This type of item needs to be rotated. Add your own ideas to this list.

Chart 9

Suggested Non-food Preparedness Items

Adhesive Tape
Aspirin
Alcohol, Rubbing
Baby Needs
   Baby Oil & Powder
Band Aids
Bandages & Gauze
   Squares
Bar B Que, Portable
Battery Radio &
   Extra Batteries
   Device for re-
   charging batteries
Blankets & Bedding
   Sheets
   Pillowcases
   Rubber sheets,
   etc.
Boric Acid
Camp Stove
Candles & candl-
   holders (or gas
   lantern & fuel)
Chemical Toilet (or
   recepticle for
   human waste)
Cleaning Supplies
   Ammonia
   Cleanser
   Clorox for dis-
   infectant & water
   purification
   Lysol Disinfectant
Clothespins
Clothing (extra)
   Coats
   Dresses
   Gloves
   Hose
   Pants

Play Clothes
Shirts
Shoes & Extra
   Laces
Socks
Sweaters
Suits
Underwear
Extra Yardage, etc.
Cold Remedies
Combs
Cooking Needs
   Can Opener
   Canned Heat (or a
   cookstove & fuel)
   Any camping
   equipment is ideal
   to have around
Cotton Balls & Q tips
Deodorant
Disposable Diapers
   (useful even if no
   baby)
Dish rags & Towels
Dishwashing Soap
Disinfectants
Epsom Salts
Egg Beater, manual
   kind
Extra Fuses
Feminine Hygiene
   items (Kotex
   would make a use-
   ful bandage pad)
First Aid Book &
   First Aid Kits (for
   car and home)
Flashlight (that works)
   & extra batteries
Foil

Large Garbage Can with
   lid (Many use new
   cans for storage)
Gauze
Grinder for wheat and
   grains
Halazone or Iodine
   Water Purification
   Tablets
Hand Lotion
Hot Water Bottle &
   Ice Bag
Iodine
Kaopectate
Kettle
Kleenex
Knives
Laxatives
Light Bulbs
Matches (in sealed
   metal container)
Milk of Magnesia
"Morale Builders" -
   (books, games)
Mouse Traps
Necessary Drugs, etc.
Ointments
Paper (grocery bags,
   newspapers & paper
   towels for sanitary
   use)
Paper Cups, Napkins &
   Plates
Pencils & Pens
Personal needs for men
   & women
Popcorn
Rags (clean, for
   bandages, etc.)
Razor Blades

Chart 1—Continued

Rope
Salt
Seeds
Sewing Supplies
  Buttons
  Needles
  Pins (safety
  & straight)
  Scissors
  Sewing machine &
  needles
  Snaps & hooks
  Thread
  Zippers
Shampoo
Sheets
  (old ones can be
  used for band-
  ages

Shaving Supplies
Soap
Soda
Tea (for tanic acid)
Toilet Tissue
Special Diet Foods
Thermometers
Tools
  Axe
  Hammer
Nails
  Pliers
  Saw
  Screw driver &
  Screws
  Shovel
Toothbrushes &
  Toothpaste
  Powder keeps

better, or use
mixture of 1/4
salt and 3/4 soda)
Toothpicks
Towels & Wash Rags
Wax Paper
Vasoline
Vitamins & Vitamin C
Washboard
Water (for emergency)
Wax Paper
Writing Paper
Foods with medicinal
  uses:
  Baking powder
  Baking soda
  Cornstarch
  Vinegar

Other non-food preparedness items which our family needs are:

_____

_____

_____

_____

_____

_____

_____

_____

_____

_____

_____

_____

_____

_____

CHAPTER III

SUGGESTIONS FOR EFFECTIVE USE OF DEHYDRATED FOODS

General Hints

Practice: Don't expect perfection the first time you prepare dried foods. If you practice and learn how to season and cook these foods properly they are very good. Start using some of these foods now, so you will know how to use them should you have the occasion to have to live with your storage supply being your only source of food.

Create New Recipes: The main dish recipes are just a few of the ways you can make edible meals for your families using items in your food storage. By interchanging meats and other ingredients you can come up with many more recipes.

Altering Recipes: Don't be afraid to work with these foods. Vary and adapt the recipes to suit your tastes. Be sure to season them according to your regular cooking habits and in conformance with your family's likes and dislikes.

Fruits and Vegetables

Dehydrated Fruit: Dehydrated fruit should not be overcooked if you are going to serve it as a fruit. The more you cook it the more mushy it will become. Dehydrated fruit can be eaten "as is" out of the can. Children especially like it.

Casseroles: In your casseroles, try interchanging a variety of noodles with macaroni, spaghetti or rice. Use a different kind each time. Even the chow mein noodles are good in casseroles.

Macaroni: Add to your regular recipe for macaroni and cheese one cup whole or cracked wheat (cooked), or one cup reconstituted textured vegetable protein, or both.

Soup or Stew: Next time you make soup or stew, add one cup of whole or cracked wheat (cooked). Make your soups of dehydrated vegetables, wheat, and barley, and season as you normally would. It's very good. Use bouillon and textured vegetable protein meats for more variety.

Tuna-Noodle Casserole: Add to your next tuna-noodle casserole one cup cooked wheat for extra body and flavor.

Cabbage Rolls: Use cooked cracked or whole wheat in your

cabbage rolls instead of rice for a tasty variety. Naturally you'd use dehydrated onions!

Dry Milk

When using dry milk in recipes in which the milk must be scalded, be sure you mix the milk well or it will settle to the bottom of the pan and burn. Make a paste first, as in gravy, then it will mix easily.

Milk is not a permanent storage item. "Instant" non-fat dry milk will store 1-1½ years. It cannot be guaranteed for freshness after this period of time. "Regular" non-fat dry milk will store longer—2-2½ years. If cared for properly, chances are it can and will keep longer, but there is no guarantee. If the milk you have stored gets hard, break it up. It's still fine for cooking.

The process of mixing "regular" dry milk with water is much easier if the water is quite warm. Measure the amount of water needed and add the milk to the water, blending it as you add the milk as you would to make a paste for gravy. It won't lump so much if you add a little milk at a time and work it in. Remember the warm water! (if you have a blender, mix your milk in it.)

For richer milk, use more dry milk—increase as much as twice, expecially for drinking purposes. To drink it "straight," add ¼ grain saccharin tablet per ½ gallon milk and stir to put the sweet back in, or even add one or two tablespoons of sugar. This will help take away the "chalk" taste.

In any recipe that calls for milk, add dry milk to the other dry ingredients, then add the proper amount of water with the liquid. Dry milk added to meat loaves, potatoes, casseroles, biscuits, pancakes, and cereals enriches the food value. (Just a thought to remember when things get rough and you still want your family well fed.)

Chart 10

Small Quantity Guide for Mixing Milk

For:		Mix:	
	1 quart milk		1 cup dry milk, 4 cups water
	1 pint milk		½ cup dry milk, 2 cups water
	1 cup milk		¼ cup dry milk, 1 cup water
	½ cup milk		2 Tb. dry milk, ½ cup water
	¼ cup milk		1 Tb. dry milk, ¼ cup water

Eggs

When adding dehydrated eggs or dry milk to the dry ingredients of a recipe, be sure to add the proper amount of liquid to the liquid ingredients.

When a recipe calls for beaten eggs, blend the eggs as suggested for the milk, mix a small amount of water to make a smooth paste, then add the remainder of water.

To measure eggs effectively, put whole egg solids in standard measuring cups of spoons a little at a time. Pack firmly and level.

For scrambled eggs, put one cup dry egg solids into bowl. Add ¼ cup dry milk. Slowly add one cup water, mixing on slow speed (or with hand whip) until mixture is perfectly smooth. Pour into greased skillet. Add seasoning to taste. Cook to desired texture while stirring constantly. For variety, add bacon bits, diced potatoes, onion, etc. (Makes about 4 servings.)

Remember, these egg products store for 2 to 2½ years. Their price makes them very practical to use in all cooking, especially when fresh egg prices soar. Dried eggs should be refrigerated after opening. For this reason many prefer to use the No. 2½ size can instead of the No. 10 can.

You realize, of course, that it's just as easy and good to fix your french toast using egg solids and dry milk as the "other" way.

To Bake with Whole Solid Eggs:

Bread, cookies—Sift egg solids with other dry ingredients. Add water as part of the liquids.

Cakes—Blend egg solids with water to use as beaten eggs. To reconstitute, use only the amount needed for the recipe. Measure the amount of egg needed and add to the water, a little at a time. (It will blend much easier if the water is warm.)

Desserts—Mix egg solids, sugar, and salt with a fork for easier mixing with water.

Chart 11

Equivalents: Shell Eggs and Dried Eggs

Shell Eggs	Amount of Whole Egg Solids	Amount of Water
1	2 Tb.	2 Tb. + 1½ tsp.
2	¼ cup	¼ cup + 1 Tb.
3	¼ cup + 2 Tb.	½ cup
4	½ cup	2/3 cup
5	½ cup + 2 Tb.	3/4 cup
6	3/4 cup	1 cup less 1 Tb.
7	3/4 cup + 2 Tb.	1 cup + 2 Tb.
8	1 cup	1¼ cup

Honey

Five types of honey are available on the market: (1) liquid

(used in most recipes); (2) granulated; (3) solid, sometimes called candied; (4) creamed or honey spread; and (5) comb or cut comb.

As a rule, the lighter the color, the milder the flavor will be. Milk flavored honey, such as clover honey, should be used in baking.

Extracted and comb honey keep best in a covered container in a dry place at room temperature (70-80° F.). The cover is necessary because honey loses aroma and flavor and absorbs moisture and odors readily when exposed to air.

Crystallization is a natural process and does not harm the honey at all. To make it liquid again, put it in a double boiler or in a container in a pan of very warm water (no warmer than your hand can bear) until the crystals go away. Don't overheat or boil. This will cause it to change color and flavor. Refrigeration will hasten crystallization. Large five-gallon cans of honey are harder to melt down than smaller cans. This should be considered in your choice of storage size.

Honey can be used, measure for measure, in place of sugar in preparing puddings, custards, pie fillings, baked apples, candied or sweet and sour vegetables, and salad dressings.

In cakes, honey can replace as much as one-half the sugar without changing the other ingredients.

In cookies, the amount of honey that can replace the sugar varies with the type of cookie. For gingersnaps, for example, replace no more than 1/3 of the sugar with honey. For brownies, honey may be used for half of the sugar called for. For fruit bars, honey can be used up to 2/3 of the sugar.

In both cakes and cookies, the honey should be mixed thoroughly with the other ingredients to prevent a soggy layer from being formed on top. Combine honey with either the shortening or the liquid.

Guide to Recipes

Charts twelve and thirteen will aid in the use of the recipes found in the remaining chapters of this book.

Chart 12

Abbreviation Key

DH	dehydrated	c.	cup
MPF	Multi-purpose Food	Pkg.	package
TVP	Textured Vegetable Protein, meat substitute	lb.	pound
Re Con	Reconstitute, replace the water in the product	qt.	quart
Gran. sugar	granulated or regular white sugar	tsp.	teaspoon
+	plus	Tb.	tablespoon

Chart 13

Ingredients needed for Recipes in This Book

A
Allspice
Almond extract
Ammonia
Apples, dh
Apple nuggets, dh
Apricots, dh

B
Baking Soda
Baking Powder
Banana flakes, dh
Barley
Bay leaves
Beans—dry, navy,
    pinto, red
Beets, dh
Biscuit mix
Bologna (optional)
Bouillon—beef,
    chicken

C
Cabbage flakes, dh
Carrots, dh
Celery seed
Cheese
Chili powder
Chocolate chips
    (optional)
Cinnamon
Clams, canned
    (optional)
Cloves
Coconut
Corn, dh
Corn meal
Cornstarch
Corn syrup
Cracklings

D
Dates, dh

E
Eggs, dh

F
Flour, white
Flour, whole wheat

Fruit Galaxy, dh
Frankfurters (optional)

G
Garlic salt
Gelatin
Ginger
Graham crackers
Grease (for soap)
Green beans, dh
Green peppers, dh

H
Honey

K
Kerosene

L
Lemon juice
Lentils
Lye

M
Macaroni
Margarine
Marjoram
Mayonnaise
Meat substitutes
    Bacon bits
    Beef granules
    Ham
    Chicken
Milk, condensed
Milk, dry
Molasses
MPF (multi-purpose
    Food)

N
Nuts (optional)
Nutmeg
Noodles

O
Oatmeal
Oil, vegetable
Olives
Onions, dh
Orange Juice
Oregano

P
Paprika
Parsley flakes
Peaches, dh
Peanut butter
Pears, dh
Peas, dh
Peas, split
Pepper
Potatoes, dh
Poultry seasoning
Prunes, dh

R
Raisins
Rice

S
Sage
Salt Shortening
Soda
Soup mix, dh
Soups (cream style)
Sour cream
Spaghetti
Spices
Spinach, dh
Stew blend
Sugar, brown
Sugar, granulated
Sugar, raw

T
Thyme
Tomato crystals, dh
TVP—see meat sub-
    stitutes

V
Vanilla
Vinegar

W
Water
Wheat
Worcestershire sauce

Y
Yams
Yeast

CHAPTER IV

RECIPES: FRUITS

Applesauce

1½ c. DH apple nuggets	½ tsp. lemon juice
2 c. water	Cinnamon and/or nut-
2 Tb. sugar	meg & allspice to taste

Combine apple nuggets and water in a saucepan; simmer 15 minutes. Stir in sugar and cook for 3 minutes. Add lemon juice and spices as to your liking. Cook to desired thickness. 4 servings.

Apricots

1 c. DH apricots	1/8 c. sugar
2 c. water	1/2 tsp. lemon juice,
	if desired

Place apricots and water in sauce pan. Bring to a boil, add sugar and lemon juice, stir until dissolved. Cool and serve.

or

Place 1 c. DH apricots and 2½ c. cold water in bowl. Cover and leave in refrigerator several hours. When ready to serve, add sugar and stir. 4-5 servings.

Date Nuggets

To reconstitute for making cookies, etc., pour approximately 1 c. boiling water over 1 c. DH   dates. Let sit 5-10 minutes. Drain and use.

Cooks fully in 5 minutes when added to hot cereal.

Fruit Galaxy

1 c. DH fruit galaxy	2 Tb. sugar
1½-2 c. water	½ tsp. lemon juice

Cover fruit with water in bowl. Let sit overnight in refrigerator. Before serving stir in sugar.

or

Cover and bring to a boil. Simmer about 5-8 minutes. Stir in sugar and cool. 4 servings.

Peaches

1 c. DH peaches	1/8 c. sugar
2 c. water	1/2 tsp. lemon juice

Prepare the same as apricots, either by cooking or soaking. About 4 servings.

Pears

1 c. DH pears	2½ Tb. sugar
2 c. water	½ tsp. lemon juice, if desired

Add pears to boiling water. Reduce heat & simmer about 20 minutes or until almost tender. Add sugar and cook a few minutes longer. Add lemon juice if desired. Remove from pan, cool and serve. 4-6 servings.

Stewed Prunes

1 c. DH prunes	¼ c. sugar
2 c. water	Lemon juice, if desired

Bring prunes and water to a boil; add sugar and simmer 5 minutes. Add lemon juice if desired. Remove from heat and cool at room temperature. 4-6 servings.

Freeze-Dried Fruits

As a basic rule of thumb, add 1 part fruit to 2 parts liquid— water, milk, cream or juice. Allow to reconstitute. Add sugar or spices to taste.

**IDEA: Have you found out what a fabulous snack and fruit for the lunch box the DH fruit is, straight from the can? Find out and then you'll have to find a good place to hide it from the family.

CHAPTER V

RECIPES: VEGETABLES

Basic Reconstitution Recipe for DH Vegetables

Add 1 cup vegetables to 2 cups boiling water. Cover and wait five minutes. Drain and season with margarine, salt and pepper, sugar, or other favorite seasonings to taste. Don't cook too long or they will become mushy. About 4 servings.

Diced Beets

1 c. DH beets	1/2 tsp. sugar
2 c. water	

Rinse, combine beets with cold water. Bring to a boil and simmer about 15-20 minutes. Season to taste and serve.

Cooked Cabbage

1/2 c. DH cabbage flakes	1 3/4 c. unsalted water
1/2 tsp. sugar, if desired	

Rinse, combine ingredients in a saucepan, bring to a boil. Turn down heat and simmer for 5-10 minutes until tender. Drain excess water. Serve with salt and pepper to taste. Dot with butter.

**Variation: Reconstitute cabbage, turn into skillet and fry in margarine or shortening for 5-7 minutes. Add ½ c. bacon bits for good flavor.

DH Diced Carrots

½ c. diced carrots	½ tsp. sugar
1 c. unsalted water	

Add carrots to cold water. Bring to a boil and simmer until

tender, about 10-20 minutes. Stir occasionally, drain and salt to taste.

Sliced Carrots

1 c. DH sliced carrots   1 tsp. sugar
2 c. unsalted water

Presoak and allow more cooking time than for diced carrots. Bring to a boil and simmer until tender, about 15-25 minutes. Stir occasionally, drain if necessary and salt.

DH Celery

Use from package in wet dishes or soak flakes in cold water for 5 minutes, drain and use. Three tsp. of celery flakes are equivalent to ½ medium-size stalk of celery. (Ratio for reconstitution: 2 Tb. celery + ¼ c. celery + ½ c. water.).

DH Sweet Corn

Soak 1 c. corn in 2½ c. water for 1 hour. Add 1 tsp. sugar, ½ tsp. salt, dash of pepper, 2 Tb. butter. Simmer 20-30 minutes. Return to stove for 2 minutes. (Also try adding bacon chips.) 4-5 servings.

DH Green Peppers

Ratio for reconstitution: 2 Tb. green pepper + ½ c. water; ¼ c. green pepper + 1 c. water.

Sliced Celery

Add dry to soups, stews, moist casseroles, etc., or reconstitute for salads, etc. ¼ c. dry @ approximately 1 c. reconstituted.

Green Beans

1 c. DH green beans	1 tsp. sugar
3 c. water	salt, pepper, margarine
	to taste

Rinse. Add beans to water, bring to a boil, then simmer about 15-20 minutes until tender.

**Variation: Add ½ c. bacon bits, ½ c. DH onions, or combine all the above with 1 can cream of mushroom soup. Place in baking dish for 20 minutes at 350°. 6 servings.

Onions

½ c. DH onions, chopped	1½ c. water
or sliced	

Rinse. Cover with water, allow to stand 10-15 minutes. Onions will expand to about 1 full cup. If onions are to be used in skillet dish or cooked, just add dry onion to mixture. (For ½ c. onions, reconstitute 2 Tb. DH onions with ½ c. water; for 1 c. onions use 1 c. water with ¼ c. DH onions.)

DH Peas

2/3 c. DH peas	½ tsp. sugar
2 c. water	Salt, pepper, margarine
	to taste

Rinse. Add peas to cold water. Bring to a boil and simmer 15-20 minutes or until tender. Season to taste. Soaking for 2 hours will reduce cooking time about ½.

Diced Potatoes

1 c. DH diced potatoes	2-3 c. cool, salted water

Rinse. Add the potatoes to cool water. Simmer in covered saucepan until tender, but not mushy, about 10-15 minutes. Stir occasionally. Drain. Use in potato salad, creamed potatoes, hash brown potatoes, potato soup, hash, casseroles, etc. (Cooking time may be cut in half by soaking for 5-10 minutes.)

Sliced Potatoes

2 c. DH diced potatoes   4 c. boiling, salted water

Rinse. Simmer 10-15 minutes until tender. (Presoaking reduces cooking time.) Add extra liquid if necessary. Use as freshly sliced potatoes.

Scalloped Potatoes

2 c. DH potato slices, or   ¼ lb. grated cheese (or
   diced   dry cheddar)
2-3 c. water   Salt and pepper to
2 Tb. margarine   taste
2 Tb. dry milk + ½ c. water   ½ c. bacon bits
1 Tb. flour   optional)
1 Tb. DH onion

Rinse and reconstitute potatoes and onions separately. Saute onion in margarine until soft, but not browned. Stir in flour, salt and pepper. Add milk, cook until smooth and thick, stirring continually. Add cheese, stir until melted. Remove from stove. Mix potatoes, bacon bits, and cheese sauce. Bake in a casserole dish 20-25 minutes at 325°.

Potato Shreds

2 c. potato shreds   6 c. boiling water

Simmer until tender, about 5-10 minutes. Keep pan covered. Add extra liquid if necessary. Season to taste and serve, or drain and hash brown. (To use for hash browns or recipes requiring further cooking, simmer only 5 minutes.)

DH Spinach

Rinse off spinach. Bring 1 c. water to a rolling boil. Add 1 c. spinach flakes and simmer about 3 minutes. Do not overcook. Drain. Add butter, salt and 1 tsp. vinegar.

**Variation: Drain and add ½ c. cream of mushroom soup and return to stove for 2 minutes.

Tomato Sauce, Paste, Juice, or Soup

Paste: 1 c. DH tomato crystals, 1 3/4 c. water, ½ tsp. sugar
Sauce: 1 c. DH tomato crystals, 3 c. water; ½ tsp. sugar
Juice: 1 c. tomato crystals; 3-5 c. water, to desired thickness, salt, pepper, lemon juice to taste
Soup: 1 c. DH tomato crystals; 3/4 c. water, ½ c. dry milk, salt and pepper to taste—and of course crackers!

Yams

2 c. DH yams   2 c. *hot* water
Seasonings to taste

Blend yams to desired consistency and serve.

Candied Yams

2 c. DH yams   2 c. boiling water
1 c. miniature marshmallows   1 tsp nutmeg
  (or ¼ c. evaporated milk   1 tsp allspice
  and ½ c. miniature marsh-   1 Tb. margarine
  mallows)   2 Tb. brown sugar

Blend together and serve or heat in oven in casserole dish for 10 minutes. To increase use equal amounts of yams and water. Season to taste.

Yam and Apple Dish

1-1½ c. DH yams	1-1½ c. water
1 c. water	½ c. brown sugar
1 tsp. salt	2 Tb. margarine

Reconstitute yam flakes using 1 c. water and salt. Arrange apple slices in bottom of greased pan. Cover with yams. Make syrup of rest of ingredients and pour over sweet potatoes. Bake at 350° for 45 minutes.

CHAPTER VI

RECIPES: MEAT SUBSTITUTES

Basic Reconstitution Recipes
(4-6 servings)

Beef Flavored Diced

Completely cover 1 c. beef dices with water or beef bouillon (to add flavor) and simmer for 15 minutes to reconstitute. Use as cooked meat.

or

Add dry to wet dishes that require further cooking and simmer for about 15 minutes or longer, but remember to add about 1 3/4 c. extra liquid for each cup of meat used.

Beef Flavored Granules

Completely cover 1 c. of beef flavored granules with water or beef bouillon (to add flavor) and simmer for 10 minutes to reconstitute. Use as cooked meat.

or

Add dry to wet dishes that require further cooking and simmer for about 10 minutes or longer, but remember to add about 1 3/4 c. extra liquid for each cup of meat used.

Burger Granules

Completely cover 1 c. burger granules with water or beef bouillon (to add flavor) and let stand a minimum of 30 minutes to reconstitute. Then add to dishes that require at least 30 minutes more simmering.

or

Completely cover 1 c. burger granules with water or beef bouillon (to add flavor) and simmer for 15 minutes to reconstitute. Use as cooked meat.

Chicken Flavored Dices

Completely cover 1 c. chicken dices with water or chicken bouillon (to add flavor). Follow directions for beef dices.

Chicken Flavored Granules

Completly cover 1 c. chicken granules with water or chicken bouillon (to add flavor). Follow directions for beef granules.

Ham Flavored Dices

Completely cover 1 c. ham dices with water or ham bouillon (to add flavor). Follow directions for beef dices.

Ham Flavored Granules

Completely cover 1 c. ham granules with water or ham bouillon (to add flavor). Follow directions for beef granules.

Beef Flavored Dices

Use in casseroles, pot pies and soups in place of stewing meat or diced meats. No work or preparation. Mix your ingredients, put in your meat and seasonings to taste. Remember not to overcook.

Beef Flavored Granules or Burger Granules

These can be used in any recipe where you would normally use ground beef. (About 1 equals 1 lb. ground beef).

Meat Loaf

Combine all your ingredients using beef flavored granules or burger granules and add sufficient water for swelling. Remember to season and cook as you normally do. It doesn't need to cook nearly as long, but long enough so the flavor and moisture are well balanced.

Spaghetti Sauce

Just put the reconstituted beef granules into the sauce and seasonings, and simmer as you normally do.

Tacos

Reconstitute TVP and onions at same time in same bowl. Then brown for a very few minutes and it's ready.

Chicken Dices

Use in casseroles, pot pies, and soups in place of stewed or diced chicken. No work or preparation. Mix your ingredients, put in your meat and seasonings to taste. Remember not to overcook.

Chicken Granules

These are better suited for making chicken loaf or sandwich spread.

Chicken Sandwich Spread

Reconstitute chicken granules and drain. Add mayonnaise, lemon juice, onion, shredded cheese, celery, green pepper, etc. to taste. Tastes better warm.

Ham Dices

If you are having ham and beans, or ham and pea soup, prepare your beans and peas as always. Put in ham dices and cook to thickness of soup you desire. Also good in potatoes au gratin or scalloped potatoes, macaroni and cheese, etc.

Ham Granules

These are better suited for making soup, ham loaf, or sandwich spread.

Ham Sandwich Spread

Reconstitute ham granules and drain. Add Mayonnaise, mustard, shredded cheese and seasonings to taste. Delicious warm.

Bacon Bits

These are ideal for cooking with eggs. Mix in before scrambling or sprinkle on top before poaching. If you still want your eggs sunnyside up, put a few bacon bits in the pan to flavor the shortening. This also works with country fried potatoes. Put a few bacon bits in the pan and it adds much flavor. (You can reconstitute dehydrated potato slices and use bacon bits very nicely!)

If you are using dry eggs, mix them well and mix some bacon bits in with the eggs.

Bacon bits added to green beans or cooked cabbage also add a nice flavor. You can also use bacon bits in making chowders and soups; as topping on vegetable salads; in egg salad sandwiches; in "bacon bits" lettuce & tomato sandwiches; etc.

CHAPTER VII

RECIPES: MAIN DISHES

Baked Beans

1 lb. small red beans
Salt to taste
½ c. DH onions +
  1½ c. water
1 tsp. chili powder

2 c. tomato crystals +
  3-4 c. water
1¼-1½ c. brown sugar
1½ c. bacon bits

Combine salt, onions and beans. Cover with water and cook 3-4 hours until skins split. Reconstitute tomato crystals to desired thickness. Add remaining ingredients; put into casserole. Bake at 275°, 5-7 hours. (Make a large batch and freeze half for a busy day.) 10-12 servings.

Beef and Dumplins

1½ c. beef TVP dices +
  1½ c. warm water
1/3 c. flour
1 tsp. garlic salt
Salt and pepper to taste

1½ c. water
1 can cream of
  chicken soup
¼ c. dry milk + 1 c. water
½ c. DH onions + 1 c. water

Reconstitute DH products. Roll meat pieces in flour and garlic salt. Brown for a few minutes. Add salt and pepper and water; simmer for 5-7 minutes. Place in a large casserole. Mix soup and milk; add onions; pour over meat.

Mix a batch of your favorite biscuit batter and drop by teaspoonful on top of the casserole. Bake at 350°, 20-25 minutes. 6 servings.

Beef TVP and Noodle Casserole

1½ c. beef TVP dices +
  1½ c. warm water

1½ c. beef bouillon (liquid)
1 Tb. paprika

3 Tb. flour
1 tsp. garlic salt
2 Tb. shortening or oil
2 Tb. DH onion + ½ c. water

Salt and pepper to taste
1-8 oz. pkg. noodles, cooked
1 Tb. margarine

Reconstitute DH products. Mix flour and garlic salt. Roll beef pieces in flour until covered. Brown beef a few minutes in shortening. Add onion; cook until tender. Add all remaining ingredients except noodles and margarine. Stir well. Simmer over low heat 15-20 minutes, stirring occasionally to prevent burning. Put cooked noodles into baking dish; pour meat mixture over them. Bake at 350° approximately 10 minutes or until well heated. 6 servings.

Beef TVP Skillet Dish

1 c. beef TVP dices or granules- cover with warm water
¼ c. DH onions + 1 c. water
¾-1 c. tomato crystals + 2 c. water
½ c. cabbage flakes + 2 c. water

1½ Tb. shortening
1 tsp. Worcestershire sauce
1 c. uncooked macaroni
Salt and pepper to taste
½ c. grated cheese (or dry cheddar)

Cover meat product and onions with water. Reconstitute other DH products, making tomato sauce to desired thickness. After reconstituting, drain excess water from vegetables and meat. Brown beef and onion in shortening. Add other ingredients except cheese. Simmer 15-20 minutes until macaroni is tender. Sprinkle cheese on top. Serve hot. 6 servings.

Beef TVP Stew

1-1½ c. beef TVP dices
1½-2 c. DH stew blend
10 c. water (approximately)
Salt, pepper and seasonings to taste

½ c. DH onion
½ c. barley
½ c. rice
3-4 Tb. flour + 1 c. water

Combine ingredients in 2 qt. kettle or sauce pan. Simmer

35-40 minutes, making sure rice and barley are cooked. Make a paste out of flour and water, mixing until smooth. Put into stew, stir until juice thickens. Serve with rolls, muffins, biscuits, or cornbread.

**Variation: Add 1 c. cooked whole or cracked wheat, or try chicken or ham TVP. About 8 servings.

Tasty Beef TVP Supper

1-8 oz. pkg. noodles
1 Tb. margarine
¼ c. dry milk + 1 c. water
1-1½ c. beef TVP dices +
   water to reconstitute

½ c. DH onions + 1½ c.
   water
Salt and pepper to taste
1 can cream of mushroom
   soup

Reconstitute DH products. Cook noodles. Brown meat a few minutes. Combine all ingredients except noodles and margarine, and simmer until smooth and creamy. Serve over buttered noodles.

**Variation: Serve over rice or cooked whole wheat. 6-8 servings.

It's Full of Boloney

1 c. DH diced potatoes +
   2 c. water
*1½ c. cut-up bologna
1 Tb. DH green pepper +
   ¼ c. water

½ c. DH cabbage flakes
6 Tb. flour
Salt and pepper to taste
3 Tb. margarine
½ c. dry milk + 2 c. water

Reconstitute DH products. Arrange potatoes, meat, green pepper, cabbage, flour, and seasoning in layers in a baking dish. Dot each layer with margarine. Pour milk over all. Bake at 350°for 1 hour. 4-6 servings.

*Try spam or ham TVP.

Cabbage and Frank Pie

2-2½ c. cabbage flakes +
   2 c. warm water
*1 pkg. frankfurters
3 Tb. brown sugar

3 Tb. lemon juice
2 Tb. margarine
Salt and pepper to taste

Reconstitute DH cabbage until just tender, then drain. Place cabbage in large pie plate or shallow casserole dish. Slit frankfurters lengthwise, cut in half crosswise and arrange attractively on cabbage, cut side down. Combine lemon juice and brown sugar, sprinkle over "pie." Dot with margarine. Bake at 400° for 5-10 minutes or until franks are brown. *Try spam or ham TVP dices. 4-5 servings.

"Cheesy" Noodle Ring

1-8 oz. pkg. noodles, cooked
1 c. shredded American
   cheese (or dry Cheddar)
½ c. soft bread crumbs
¾ c. dry milk + 1½ c.
   water
1 Tb. DH parsley flakes +
   1/8 c. water

¼ c. egg solids + ¼ c. and
   1 Tb. water, beaten
   (to equal 2 eggs)
Salt and pepper to taste
2 Tb. chopped pimiento
2 Tb. DH celery + ¼ c.
   water

Reconstitute DH products. Scald milk. Mix all ingredients well. Put into greased mold or ring. Put mold in a pan of water and bake 30-35 minutes at 350°. Fill center with creamed tuna, chicken or beef (TVP of course!) 6 servings.

Chicken TVP—Corn Casserole

2 c. chicken TVP dices +
   2 c. warm water
½ c. tomato crystals +
   1 c. water, blended
1 Tb. lemon juice
¼ c. egg solids + ¼ c. and
   1 Tb. warm water,
   mix (to equal 2 eggs)
1 c. crushed corn chips
Salt and pepper to taste

½ c. DH corn, cooked +
   1 c. water
1 tsp Worcestershire Sauce
2 Tb. DH celery +
   ¼ c. water
1 Tb. DH onion +
   ½ c. water
1 c. shredded American
   cheese (or dry Cheddar)

Reconstitute DH products. Mix all ingredients except cheese. Put into a baking dish. Bake at 350° for 40 minutes. Remove from oven and sprinkle top with cheese. Return for 10 minutes longer.

Chicken TVP—Noodle Casserole

1½ c. chicken TVP dices +
   1½ c. warm water
Salt and pepper to taste
½ c. DH peas + about 1½
   c. water
½ c. DH carrots + 1 c. water
2 Tb. DH green pepper +
   ½ c. water

¼ c. DH celery + ½ c. water
½ lb. noodles, cooked
   (or 2 c. cooked rice)
2 Tb. DH onion +
   ½ c. water
Chicken broth (can be
   made from bouillon)

Reconstitute dehydrated products. Mix all ingredients except broth together. Add broth until mixture is very moist. Bake at 325° for 1 hour. (In a recipe such as this one, put all the vegetables in one bowl to reconstitute.) 5-6 servings

Chicken TVP—Rice Casserole

2/3 c. chicken TVP dices +
   liquid to reconstitute
3+ c. boiling water
1/2-2/3 c. uncooked rice
1 pkg. dry chicken &
   noodle, or rice soup mix
   (or make soup broth)

1 Tb. DH onion (or 1 pkg.
   dry soup mix)
1 Tb. DH green pepper
2 Tb. DH celery
Slivered almonds, if desired
Marjoram, sage, poultry
   seasoning to taste

Cover chicken dices well with water (or chicken bouillon to add flavor) and simmer for about 15 minutes to reconstitute. Drain. Bring water to a boil. Add all ingredients and boil for 5 minutes only. It will be soupy. Bake for 1 hour at 350° in casserole dish. 5-6 servings

Chicken and Rice Ring

1 c. chicken TVP dices +
   1 c. warm water
1 c. soft bread crumbs
¾ c. cooked rice
Salt and pepper to taste
2 Tb. DH onion + ¼ c. water
¼=¾ c. dry milk + 1¼-1¾ c.
   water

1 Tb. DH green pepper +
   ¼ c. water
¼ c. chopped pimiento
   (optional)
¼ c. egg solids + ¼ c. and
   1 Tb. water, beaten (to
   equal 2 eggs)
¼ c. margarine

Reconstitute DH products. Combine all ingredients and press into ring mold. Bake 40-50 minutes at 350°. Unmold and fill center with colorful cooked vegetables.

**Variation: Press into muffin tins or custard cups for individual servings. Reduce baking time. Try adding ½ c. chopped nuts.
4-6 servings

Hot Chicken Salad

2 c. chicken TVP dices +
   2 c. warm water
¼ c. DH celery + ½ c. water
1 Tb. DH green pepper +
   ¼ c. water
½ c. mayonnaise or
   salad dressing
3 Tb. pimiento, cut in
   small strips

2 Tb. minced DH onion +
   ½ c. water
1 tsp. salt
2 Tb. lemon juice
1/3 c. shredded sharp or
   swiss cheese (or dry
   cheddar)
3 c. coarsely broken
   potato chips

Reconstitute DH products. Blend ingredients, except cheese and potato chips, in greased 1½ qt. baking dish. Sprinkle cheese, then potato chips over top. Bake at 350° for 25-30 minutes, until cheese is lightly browned and bubbly. 6-8 servings

Chili

2 c. (1 lb.) dry pinto beans
2 qts.+ water
1 c. beef TVP granules
2 c. tomato crystals

Chili powder to taste
Salt and pepper to taste
1 Tb. garlic salt
¾ c. DH onions

Cover beans with 2 qts. boiling water and let stand 50 minutes (or let soak overnight in cold water). Add beef granules and all other ingredients. Bring to a brisk boil and simmer for 2-3 hours, until done. 4-6 servings

Corn-Tomato Casserole

1 c. tomato crystals +
   2 c. water

Salt and pepper to taste
   to taste

¾ c. DH corn + 2 c. water
  (cook about 15 min.)
¼ c. DH onions + 1 c. water
¼ c. DH green peppers +
  1 c. water

1 Tb. margarine or
  shortening
1 c. dry bread crumbs
2 Tb. grated cheese (or dry
  cheddar)

Reconstitute dehydrated vegetables. Combine with seasonings in a casserole dish. Dot with margarine, sprinkle cheese and crumbs over top. Bake at 375° for 30-35 minutes.

Ham TVP—Cheese Casserole

1-5 oz. pkg. narrow noodles
  or spaghetti
1 c. ham TVP dices + 1 c.
  warm water
2 c. grated cheese (or dry
  cheddar.
1-4 oz. can sliced mushrooms

2 Tb. DH onions + ¼ c.
  water
3 Tb. DH green pepper +
  ½ c. water
1/3-½ c. tomato crystals +
  1 c. or more water—to
  desired thickness

Reconstitute dehydrated products. Cook noodles as directed on package. Drain well. Combine ham dices, cheese, mushrooms, onions, and green pepper. Alternate layers of noodles and ham mixture in greased 3 qt. casserole dish. Pour tomato mixture over layers in casserole. Bake at 350° for 30-35 minutes.

Ham TVP—Rice Skillet Dish

1 Tb. DH green pepper +
  ¼ c. water
1 Tb. DH onion + ½ c. water
  Shortening

1 c. ham TVP dices + 1 c.
  warm water
4 c. cooked rice (2 c. dry)
  Seasoning to taste

Reconstitute DH products. Brown green pepper and onion in shortening. Do not allow to get too brown—just until tender. Add ham and brown for a few minutes. Now add rice and seasonings. Cook just until rice is heated thoroughly and flavor is blended, approximately 10-15 minutes. Serve with Worcestershire sauce or soy sauce. 6 servings.

Scalloped Ham and Potatoes

½ square margarine
4 Tb. flour
    Salt and pepper to taste
¼-½ c. dry milk + 2 c. water
1½ c. DH diced potatoes
    + 4 c. water

½ c. ham TVP dices + 1½ c.
    water
½ c. grated cheese (or dry
    cheddar)

Reconstitute DH products. Combine milk, butter, flour, and salt to make a white sauce. Cook until smooth. Layer ham, potatoes, and cheese in casserole dish. Pour sauce over this evenly. Bake 45 minutes at 300°. 6 servings.

Meat Loaf

1½ c. beef TVP granules or
    burger granules + 1½ c.
    warm water
2 Tb. DH onion + ½ c. water
2 Tb. dry eggs + 2½ Tb. water
    (to equal 1 egg)
1 c. oatmeal or ½ c. cooked
    cracked wheat

1 c. tomato crystals + 2-3 c.
    water
¼ c. soup mix or 1 Tb.
    bouillon
1¼ c. MPF and seasoning
    to taste

Mix well and bake in loaf pan for 1 hour at 350°. (You will have to remember TVP products do not have the moisture of fresh meat. Work with this until it holds together for you.) 6 servings.

Tamale Pie

1 c. corn meal
1 c. cold water
3 c. boiling water
1½ tsp. salt
½ c. TVP granules + ½ c.
    warm water
2 Tb. DH onions + ¼ c. water

1 tsp. salt
    Pepper to taste
1 can chili con carne
½ c. chopped ripe olives
½ c. grated cheese (or dry
    cheddar)

Cover beef granules with warm water, and reconstitute onions.

Mix corn meal with cold water; add boiling water and 1½ tsp. salt. Cook over low heat 20 minutes, stirring occasionally.

Brown beef granules and onion in skillet; add salt & pepper and chili con carne. Stir olives into corn meal. Using 2/3 of corn meal mix, line a greased casserole dish. Fill with beef mixture and cover with the remaining corn meal. Sprinkle cheese on top. Bake 15-25 minutes at 350° in order to heat thoroughly. About 6 servings.

Cracked Wheat with Chicken Flavor

¾ c. cracked wheat, uncooked	2 c. water
¼ c. butter or margarine	1 Tb. chicken soup base,
¼ c. DH onion + 1 c. water	or 1 Tb. powdered
Seasonings to taste	bouillon (1 cube)

Place cracked wheat on sheet cake pan in oven at 350° about 10-15 minutes. Add butter and onions to wheat. Dissolve the bouillon or soup base in water. Add broth and seasoning to mixture. Put in covered casserole dish and bake at 350° for 25-30 minutes. Remove cover and stir; cook for 15 minutes more. Stir again before serving.

Could be served with gravy and meat balls or meat loaf. 4-6 servings.

Wheat and Corn Casserole

1 c. beef TVP granules + 1-1½ c. water	2 pkg. onion soup mix
1 Tb. oil or shortening	2-3 c. cooked cracked wheat (1-1½ c. dry wheat)
½ c. DH celery + ½-1 c. water	½ c. DH corn + 1-1½ c. water
½ c. DH onions + 1 c. water	Seasonings to taste
4 c. boiling water	

Rinse and reconstitute DH products. Brown meat, onions, and celery in oil; add water and soup mix. Simmer until celery becomes tender. Add corn, wheat and seasonings. Place in casserole dish and bake at 350° for 45 minutes. 10 servings.

Wheat and Meat Casserole

1 c. beef TVP dices + 1 c.
  water
½ c. DH onions + 1½ c.
  water
½ c. DH green pepper +
  1½ c. water
6 Tb. uncooked cracked
  wheat or whole wheat
  (soaked)

Worcestershire sauce,
  dash or two
2 Tb. brown sugar
1 c. tomato crystals +
  1½-2 c. water—to
  desired thickness
Cheese, grated, if
  desired

Reconstitute meat and vegetables. Brown meat in very hot grease. In a casserole dish, add alternating layers of meat, onion, peppers, and wheat. Salt, pepper, and season each layer to your taste. Blend Worcestershire sauce, brown sugar, and tomato crystals to make sauce. Cover well with tomato sauce. Bake at 350° for 45 minutes. Top with grated cheese before serving, if desired. (Try chicken or ham TVP for variety.) 6 servings.

Wheat and Meat Skillet Dish

*1½-2 c. whole or cracked
  wheat (¾ c. dry wheat)
1 c. beef TVP (cover with
  1 c. warm water)
¼-½ c. DH onions (to taste) +
  1-2 c. water
Salt, pepper, and seasonings
  to taste

1 c. tomato crystals +
  3 c. water & ½ tsp.
  sugar
2 Tb. DH green peppers +
  ¼ c. water
2 Tb. DH celery + ¼ c.
  water

Rinse and reconstitute DH products. Brown meat or TVP a few minutes; add sauce and other ingredients. Simmer 20-25 minutes.
    * You can use whole wheat left over from cereal in the morning, or soak wheat through the day.
    **Variation: Use rice in place of wheat. 4-5 servings.

Wheat Type Spaghetti

1½-2 c. beef TVP granules +
  warm water

1 bay leaf, crushed
1 tsp. parsley leaves

¼ c. DH celery + ½ c. water
½ c. DH onion + 1½ c.
   water
1 tsp. garlic salt
2 c. Tomato crystals +
   3-4 c. water
Salt and pepper to taste

1 tsp. oregano
½ tsp. marjoram
1 c. cooked cracked or
   whole wheat
¾ c. grated cheese
(Cooked spaghetti
   and cheese)

Reconstitute DH products, with tomato crystals in a separate bowl. (If you have a blender, tomato sauce is very easy to do, putting all of the spices in at the same time.) Brown beef granules for a very few minutes. Sprinkle with garlic salt. Add tomato sauce, wheat, vegetables, and spice. Add cheese, stirring until melted and thoroughly blended. Simmer 15-20 minutes, stirring occasionally to prevent burning. Serve over boiled spaghetti. About 10 servings.

Spanish Wheat

2 c. beef TVP + 2 c. water
¼=½ c. DH celery + 1 c.
   water
¼-½ c. DH chopped onion
   + ¾-1 c. water
¼ c. DH green peppers +
   ½ c. water
1 tsp garlic salt

1 tsp. chili powder, if
   desired
1½ c. tomato crystals +
   2-3 c. water
3-4 c. cooked cracked
   wheat (1½-2 c. dry
   wheat
Salt and pepper to taste

Rinse and reconstitute beef granules, green pepper, onions, and celery. Brown meat a very few minutes; add celery, onion, and green pepper plus chili powder and garlic salt. Cook until vegetables are about half done. Add tomato crystals and water; stir until well blended. Simmer about 30 minutes. Add wheat, salt and pepper. Put in casserole dish and bake 30 minutes at 350°. 10 servings.

Wheat Tamale Pie

¾ c. uncooked fine cracked
   wheat
4-4½ c. water
¾-1 c. tomato crystals

¼ c. DH green peppers +
   1 c. water
1/8 tsp. garlic salt
1 tsp. chili powder, if desired

1 c. beef TVP granules +
1 c. warm water
½ c. DH chopped or sliced
onions + 1½ c. water

Salt and pepper to taste
½ c. chopped ripe olives
½ c. cheddar cheese
(or dry cheddar)

Cook wheat in boiling water until thick. Add tomato crystals. Stir well and set aside. Brown meat, onion, and green pepper. Add remaining ingredients except cheese. Add wheat and tomato sauce mix. Put in baking dish and bake 45-50 minutes at 350°. During last 10 minutes, put cheese on top.

CHAPTER VIII

RECIPES: MULTI-PURPOSE FOOD

General Information about MPF:

Multi-purpose Food is a soybean derivative, precooked and ready to use. It is an emergency meal or a good supplement or a food extender—manufactured for foreign aid. It keeps indefinitely. One ounce—3 tablespoons—of MPF adds 14 grams of high quality protein plus a generous amount of 12 essential vitamins and minerals to a serving of food—but only 75 calories. (1/3 cup MPF provides 1/3 of the required protein, minerals, and vitamins, except Vitamin C.) Protein is usually obtained from meat, milk, eggs, and cheese. Since these foods are difficult to store, it follows that any emergency diet may be seriously lacking in high quality protein. If MPF is included in an emergency supply you give meat values, plus vitamins and minerals to non-meat dishes. It blends well with other foods and provides many of the essential nutrients that are often lacking in them. If MPF were eaten alone, about 15 cents worth a day, it would provide all the nutrients an adult would need. It is also an excellent year-round food supplement.

Increase liquid 2 cups for each cup of MPF used.

Recipes with Multi-purpose Food

Beverages: Blend 2 level Tb. of MPF with a large glass (8 oz.) of tomato juice, or fruit juice, milk or broth. (Make your own "Instant Breakfast")

Breads: Substitute ¼ c. MPF and ¾ c. flour for 1 c. flour.

Cereal: Blend 4 level Tb. of non-fat dry milk with 1 cup (8 oz.) of cold water. Pour over ¼ c. MPF in a bowl. Sprinkle 1 Tb. brown sugar over surface, or add honey or fruit for sweetening.

or

Combine 3 Tb. dry MPF with ½ c. cooked or ready-to-eat cereal.

Fruit:	Combine 3 Tb. dry MPF with 1 c. fruit sauce (peach, pear, apple, strawberry, rhubarb, pineapple, apricot, etc.)
Gelatin:	Moisten 1/3 c. dry MPF and 1 package (3½ oz.) apple-flavored gelatin with 2/3 c. cold pineapple juice; makes instant jellied pudding high in protein.
Hot Dish:	Add 1 c. (8 oz.) hot water to ½ c. MPF. Season with 1 Tb. soy sauce, or use catsup, gravy, steak sauce, etc.
Ice Cream:	To increase protein content and lower calorie content, combine 1/3 c. dry MPF with 1 pint softened ice cream. Harden in freezer.
Meat Loaf, Meat Balls, Meat Pat-ties:	An excellent extender-fortifier, MPF contributes to extra yield and nutrient content per slice. Combine ¾ c. dry MPF and 1½ c. liquid (water, milk, tomato juice, or soup) with 2 lbs. ground meat. Season to taste.
Pancakes & waffles:	Add ¼ c. MPF for each cup pancake mix or flour and add sufficient extra liquid to give desired consistency.
Peanut but-ter Spread:	To increase protein content and lower calorie content, combine 1/3 c. dry MPF with ½ c. peanut butter.
Sauce:	Stir 2 level Tb. MPF into ½ c. applesauce. Serve hot or cold.
Soup:	Dissolve 1 bouillon cube in a cup of hot water, stir in 2 level Tb. MPF; or, combine 3 Tb. dry MPF with 1 cup soup.
Topping:	Sprinkle on desserts, cereals, salads, pudding, hot dishes, and casseroles.

CHAPTER IX

RECIPES: SALADS

Apple Gelatin

Add ½ c. applesauce nuggets and ½ c. gelatin dessert to 1 c. boiling water. Stir until dissolved. Add 1 c. cold water. Place in refrigerator until set.

**Variations: Add chopped celery, grated cheese, cabbage, or nuts. Also try using dates in place of apples.

Cole Slaw

1 c. DH cabbage flakes	3 c. *cold* water
½ tsp. celery seed	½ tsp. sugar
(optional)	

Cover tightly and soak in refrigerator one-half hour. Drain if necessary. Serve with favorite cole slaw dressing, or one of the following:

Cole Slaw Dressings

½ c. mayonnaise	2 tsp. sugar
2 tsp. vinegar	1 tsp. salt

* * *

½ c. mayonnaise	½ c. water
3-4 Tb. sugar	½ tsp. salt
¼ c. dry milk	

Carrot and Raisin Salad

1 c. DH diced carrots	½ tsp. sugar
½ c. raisins	2 c. water

Cover with *cold* water and soak 30 minutes or overnight in refrigerator. Drain and use with favorite dressing.

**IDEA: Use various DH fruits or vegetables in gelatin salads. 1 c. fruit + 1 c. water for average 6 oz. pkg. or family size bowl of gelatin. Reconstitute fruit and drain well before adding to salad.

CHAPTER X

RECIPES: SOUPS

Bean Chowder

¾ c. dry beans
3 c. water
¾ c. diced dry potatoes
3 Tb. DH onion
1½ tsp. flour

½ c. tomato crystals +
¾ c. water
Salt to taste
Bacon bits to taste
1½ c. reconstituted
non-fat milk

Soak beans overnight in water. Do not drain. Next day, cook until tender—4-5 hours. Add potatoes and onions. Mix flour, tomato juice, salt, and bacon bits. Add to bean mixture. Cook 30 minutes, stirring occasionally to prevent sticking. Stir in milk, reheat, and serve.

Bean, Pea, or Lentil Soup

Cover 1 c. beans, peas, or lentils with 6 c. boiling water. Cover and let stand 50 minutes. Add salt, pepper, and butter to taste. Bring to a brisk boil and simmer until done—about 2-3 hours.
**Variations: Add ham TVP, carrots, onions, potatoes, tomato crystals, celery, green pepper, etc.

Clam or Fish Chowder

1 can minced clams or
1-1½ lbs. filet of sole
½ c. bacon bits
1 c. DH diced potatoes
(be sure to rinse off)
½ c. DH onion slices +
1 c. water

2 qts. water
¾ c. dry milk
Salt and pepper, seasonings
to taste (sometimes a
piece of bay leaf)

Reconstitute DH onion. Put clams (with juice from can) or fish, broken up small, in large sauce pan in water. While fish is starting to cook, saute bacon bits and onions for a few minutes. (Try not to get onions too brown.) Add bacon, onions, and potatoes and seasoning to fish. Simmer 25-30 minutes. Then bring to a boil, add milk, stir well for about one minute. Remove from heat and serve.

**Variation: Also add ¾-1 cup of tomato crystals and/or ½ cup diced DH carrots. 4-5 servings.

Green Pea Soup

2 c. (1 lg. pkg.) split peas	Pepper or other favorite
4 Tb. DH carrots	spices
4 Tb. DH celery	½ c. ham TVP dices, or ½ c.
2 Tb. DH onion	bacon bits TVP
4 qts. water	¼ tsp. thyme, if desired
2 tsp. salt	¼ tsp. marjoram to taste

Rinse and soak peas and DH vegetables overnight in the water. Do not drain. Add all spices and ham TVP. Cook until flavor is well blended, approximately one hour. Press through a sieve to desired thickness. Makes a large batch.

Vegetable Soup

DH Soup Mix or Stew Blend	Seasonings to taste
(1-1½ c. should serve 4-6)	1 cube or Tb. beef bouillon
4-5 c. water (to desired	½ c. beef chunks or beef
thickness)	TVP dices

Combine ingredients in large sauce pan. Simmer 20-30 minutes until vegetables are tender and flavors well blended.

**Variations:

—Drop biscuit dough by teaspoonfuls on top, for dumplings. Cook these 10 minutes covered, 10 minutes uncovered.

—Add 1 cup barley, rice, cooked whole or cracked wheat, or macaroni. Cook 10 to 15 minutes longer if uncooked rice or barley is used.

CHAPTER XI

RECIPES: HONEY

Honey Apple Crisp

¾ c. DH apple slices +
    2 c. water
2 Tb. sugar
1½ tsp. lemon juice
¼ c. liquid honey

¼ c. flour
2 Tb. brown sugar
1/8 tsp. salt
2 Tb. butter or margarine

Reconstitute DH apple slices by putting in water and bringing to a boil. Place apples in a shallow baking dish. Combine sugar, lemon juice and honey. Spread over apples. Combine dry ingredients; work in margarine until mixture is crumbly. Cover apples with flour mixture and bake at 375° for 30-40 minutes, until apples are tender and crust is brown. Can be topped with whipped cream, or dry milk whipped topping. 4 servings.

Honey-Date Bars

1 c. honey
3 eggs, beaten (¼ c. + 2 Tb.
    dry eggs + ½ c. water)
1 tsp. vanilla
1 1/3 c. sifted whole wheat
    flour

¼ tsp. salt
1 tsp. baking powder
1½ c. DH dates
1 c. chopped nuts
Fine granulated sugar

Mix honey, eggs and vanilla; beat well. Add sifted dry ingredients, dates, and nuts. Spread in greased 9 x 13 pan. Bake at 350° about 45 minutes. Cool in pan. Cut in 3 x 1 inch bars; roll in sugar.

Honey-Raisin Cookies

½ c. shortening
1/3 c. liquid honey

½ tsp. baking powder
¼ tsp. soda

¼ c. egg solids + ¼ c. & 1 Tb. water
1¼ c. flour
½ tsp. nutmeg
¼ tsp. salt
2/3 c. seedless raisins
¼ tsp. vanilla

Cream shortening and honey thoroughly. Mix egg solids with dry ingredients. Sift together dry ingredients. Add to creamed mixture, stir well. Add liquid, vanilla, and raisins. Mix. Drop batter by spoonful on a greased cookie sheet, 2 inches apart. Bake for 12 minutes at 350°. Makes about 2 dozen.

Honey-Bread Pudding

1 2/3 c. day-old bread cubes
¼ c. honey
2 Tb. butter or margarine
1/8 tsp. salt
2 eggs beaten (¼ c. dry eggs + ¼ c. & 1 Tb. water)
½ tsp. vanilla
1 2/3 c. hot milk (¾ c. dry milk + 1 2/3 c. water)

Reconstitute eggs and milk. Place bread in small baking dish. Combine honey, margarine, salt, eggs, and vanilla. Slowly stir in milk. Pour mixture over bread. Set dish in a pan of hot water and bake at 350° for 30-40 minutes until pudding is set. 4 servings.

Honey-Date Rice Pudding

2 c. cooked rice (about 2/3 c. uncooked)
¼ c. honey
¼ c. DH date nuggets + 1 c. water
1 tsp. grated lemon rind
¼ c. dry milk + 1 c. water
¼ c. egg solids + ¼ c. & 1 Tb. water

Reconstitute dates, eggs, and milk. Mix first four ingredients in 1 qt. casserole dish. Combine milk and eggs, pour over top. Set in pan of hot water. Bake 50-60 minutes at 350° until pudding is set. Serve warm or cold. 4-6 servings.

Honey Sandwich Fillings

Of course you're aware that honey and peanut butter go

together, besides being very good for you. Try these:

Honey and Cream Cheese Filling

3 Tb. liquid or creamed honey
1-4 oz. pkg. cream cheese

Beat honey and cream cheese together until light and fluffy. Makes 1¼ cups.

Honey Butter

Mix equal parts of crystallized honey and butter or margarine.

**IDEA: Honey with dried fruits and chopped nuts. Honey and chopped or grated orange peel.*

CHAPTER XII

RECIPES: DESSERTS

Basic Reconstitution Recipe for Using Gelatin Dessert

Scant ½ c. gelatin   1 c. cold water
1 c. hot water   (or ½ tray ice cubes)

Mix gelatin with hot water. Add cold water or ice and mix well. Set. 4-6 servings.

Fruit Gelatin

Any of your recipes calling for fruit, peaches, apricots, or apples may be interchanged, using the same measured amount. For regular recipes use ½-¾ c. fruit + 1-1½ c. water. Reconstitute and drain before adding to jello.

When fruit nuggets are used, apple or date nuggets are measured the same. Try changing them for a new taste. Use ¾ c. fruit + 1 c. water. Reconstitute and drain before adding to jello— or for thicker jello, add fruit plain to the jello.

Apple Brown Betty

2½ c. DH apple slices   ¼ c. melted butter or
5 c. water   margarine
1½ Tb. lemon juice   1 c. packed brown sugar
½ c. raisins   1 Tb. cinnamon
2 c. dry bread cubes   ¼ tsp. salt

Stir apple slices into water and bring to a boil. Remove from heat and add lemon juice and raisins. Cool. Pour melted butter over the dry bread cubes. Stir sugar, cinnamon, and salt into apples. Spread apple slices and juice in layers alternately with bread crumb mixture in 8 x 8 x 2 inch pan. Bake at 350° for about 45 minutes.

Apple Crisp

3 c. DH apple slices	*Topping:*
4 c. water	1 c. gran. sugar
1 c. gran. sugar	1 c. all-purpose flour
1¾ tsp. cinnamon	½ tsp. salt
1½ tsp. salt	½ c. soft butter or margarine

Bring apple slices to a boil in water. Remove from heat. Mix sugar, cinnamon, and salt, and stir into apple slices. Spread mixture in 8 x 8 x 2 inch pan. Sift remaining sugar, flour, and salt. Cut in butter until mixture is as fine as corn meal. Spread as topping over apple slices. Bake at 400° for about 30 minutes. Serve warm or cold with milk or cream if desired.

**Variation: Half the flour may be substituted with non-fat dry milk. Also try using applesauce as part of the filling for a tarter flavor.

Aplets (candy)

2½ tsp. gelatin	2 c. sugar
1¼ c. unsweetened applesauce	1 c. chopped nuts
(using DH apple nuggets)	1 tsp. vanilla

(To make the applesauce, mix 1¼ c. apple nuggets and 1½ c. water, cook for 15-20 minutes, and cool for use.)

Soak gelatin in ½ c. cold applesauce for 10 minutes. Combine ¾ c. applesauce with sugar and boil 10 minutes. Add gelatin mixture and boil 15 minutes, stirring constantly. Cool slightly; add nuts and vanilla. Pour into greased pan. Set until firm. Cut in squares and roll in sifted powdered sugar.

**Variation: DH apricots may be used in place of apple nuggets.

Peach Cobbler

4 c. DH peach slices	*Topping:*
7 c. water	2½ c. biscuit mix
1 c. sugar	8 Tb. margarine
½ c. cornstarch	8 Tb. sugar
½ c. cold water	1-1½ c. water
	Cinnamon and ginger, to taste

Bring the water to a boil and add the peach slices and sugar. Cook until softened. Make a paste with cornstarch and cold water and add to desired consistency. Add cinnamon and ginger, if desired. Pour into 9 x 13 inch baking dish.

Mix ingredients for topping to consistency of cake batter and spread on top of the peach mixture. Bake at 350° about 20 minutes.

Other fruits could be used for variety.

Baked Custard

¾-1 c. dry milk + 3 c. water   1/3 c. sugar
¼ c. + 2 Tb. dry egg solids +   1 tsp. vanilla
   ½ c. water (to equal 3 eggs)   Nutmeg and cinnamon
¼ tsp. salt   to taste

Scald milk. Combine egg solids, salt, and sugar; blend with water. Stir into hot milk, very slowly. Add vanilla. Pour into greased custard cups. Put in shallow pan of water. Bake at 350° for 30-40 minutes. Chill before serving. Spices may be sprinkled on top before baking. 6 servings.

Fruit Tapioca

1¼-1½ c. DH fruit galaxy (or   1/8 tsp. salt
   peaches, apples, apricots)   ¾ c. sugar
2½-3 c. water   ¼ c. tapioca, quick cooking

Mix fruit, sugar, salt, and water. Cook 10-15 minutes, stirring. Add tapioca, stir well, allow to stand for 5 minutes. Bring to a boil, stirring, so it won't burn. Serve warm or chilled. 6 servings.

Rice-Apricot Custard

2 c. water   ¼ c. dry milk + ¾ c. water
2 Tb. butter or margarine   ½ tsp. salt
1/3 c. rice   ½ c. gran. sugar
½ c. DH apricots   2 Tb. dry eggs + 2½ Tb. wa-
½ tsp. cornstarch   ter, beaten (to equal 1 egg)

Place butter in water and bring to a boil. Add rice gradually and stir well. Cover and simmer 15 minutes. Stir in DH apricots, then cover and simmer 10 more minutes

Mix cornstarch in milk; add salt, sugar, and beaten egg. Add to fruit mixture and stir continually. Cook very slowly until mixture thickens. Pour into sherbet glasses, cool and serve. 6 servings.

Fruit Crumble

2-3 c. DH fruit galaxy	¼ c. sugar
3 c. water	2 Tb. cornstarch
1½ Tb. lemon juice	½ c. water

Simmer DH fruit in water 5 minutes, then remove from heat. Stir in lemon juice and sugar. Mix cornstarch in water and add to above mixture. Cook until thick and clear, then pour into 8 x 8 in baking pan.

Topping

1 c. gran. sugar	2 Tb. dry egg + 2½ Tb. water,
2 c. all-purpose flour	beaten (to equal 1 egg)
¾ tsp. salt	1/3 c. melted butter or
1 tsp. baking powder	margarine
	Cinnamon, as needed

(Make while fruit is cooling.) Sift sugar, flour, salt, and baking powder together. Add beaten egg and mix to crumb consistency. Top cooked fruit with crumbs. Spread melted butter and cinnamon on crumb topping. Bake at 375° for 30-35 minutes.

**Variation: Half the flour may be substituted with non-fat dry milk.

Fruit Scones

¾ c. DH apple, apricot or	½ c. water
peach slices	1/3 c. gran. sugar

Bring fruit and water to a boil; reduce heat and simmer gently for 10 minutes. Remove from heat and stir in sugar. Cool.

Dough

¾ c. all-purpose flour
3 Tb. dry milk +
   1/3 c. water
2 tsp. baking powder

½ tsp. salt
1½ Tb. gran. sugar
¼ c. shortening
¾ c. quick-cooking oats

Sift flour, dry milk, baking powder, salt, and sugar together. Cut in shortening until consistency of coarse crumbs. Add rolled oats and mix lightly. Add water gradually, mixing until dough can be formed into a ball. Knead slightly on floured board and roll to 1/8 inch thickness. Cut into five inch circles (drinking glass may be used as cutter). Place approximately one teaspoonful of filling at one end of each half circle. Make a slash in the other end and fold over filling. Seal by pressing edges with fork. Brush tops with melted butter and sprinkle with sugar. Bake on ungreased cookie sheet at 425° for 15-18 minutes.

Apple Pie Filling

1 2/3 c. DH apple slices
2½ c. water
2 Tb. cornstarch
½ c. sugar

¼ tsp. salt
¼ tsp. cinnamon
1 tsp. lemon juice

Combine all ingredients and blend well. Heat to a rolling boil, stirring occasionally. Pour into pastry lined 8 or 9 inch pie pan. Top with pastry and bake at 425° for 35-40 minutes, or until apples are tender. Makes 1 pie.

Apricot or Peach Pie Filling

1 c. DH apricots or peaches
2 c. water
¼ c. cornstarch

½ c. sugar
½ tsp. salt
2 tsp. lemon juice, if desired

Add fruit to water and stir in cornstarch. Heat to a rolling boil, stirring frequently. Add sugar, salt, and lemon juice. Stir until dissolved. Cool. Fill pies and bake at 425° for 35-40 minutes. Makes 1 pie.

Basic Pudding Mixes

Basic Mix

2½ c. non-fat dry milk   1¼ c. flour
1½ c. sugar   1 tsp. salt

Mix all ingredients and store in a covered container. (Prepare as directed in individual recipes.)

Vanilla Pudding

1¼ c. Basic Mix   1 tsp. vanilla
2½ c. warm water   2 Tb. dry egg + 2½ Tb.
1 Tb. butter or margarine   water, beaten (to
                            equal 1 egg)

In top of double boiler, combine basic mix with warm water. Place over boiling water, cooking and stirring until it thickens. Cover and cook 10 minutes. Stir several times. Add margarine and remove from heat. With a spoon, beat half the mix into egg, then stir into mixture in double boiler. Cook, stirring, over hot, not boiling, water one minute. Remove from heat and stir in vanilla. Cool, stirring once or twice, then chill.

(Double boiler must be used or pudding will be too thick and gummy.)

Butterscotch Pudding

Same as Basic Mix, except substitute dark brown sugar for granulated.

Chocolate Pudding

Same as recipe for vanilla puding, except stir in 3 Tb. cocoa before cooking.

Coconut Cream

Add ½-1 c. flaked coconut to cooked vanilla, chocolate, or butterscotch pudding.

Creamy Rice Pudding

Prepare vanilla pudding recipe. Remove from heat and stir in 2 c. cooked rice.

Fruit Pudding

Prepare vanilla recipe. Chill and serve on any fresh fruit, or reconstituted or cooked DH fruit.

Apple Refrigerator Pudding

1 c. DH apple nuggets   1 lb. graham cracker
4 c. water   crumbs
1 c. brown sugar   ¼ lb. butter or margarine

Combine apple nuggets, water and brown sugar. Mix graham cracker crumbs with heated butter. Place a thick layer of the crumb mixture in the bottom of a greased 9 x 13 pan and pat firm. Cover with applesauce mixture and top with remainder of the graham cracker crumbs. Allow to stand overnight in refrigerator.
**Variation: Try using peaches in this recipe for a good-tasting change. 12 servings.

Upside Down Apricot Pudding

2 c. all-purpose flour   1 1/8 c. gran. sugar
2/3 c. gran. sugar   1/3 c. butter or margarine
4 tsp. baking powder   ¾ c. DH apricots
½ tsp. salt   1½ c. water
½-¾ c. dry milk + 1½ c. water

Sift dry ingredients together twice. Add milk and stir well. Spread batter evenly into greased 9 x 9 in. baking pan. Combine water and apricots and bring to a boil. Add sugar and margarine, and bring back to a boil. Spread apricot sauce thinly over batter in baking pan. Bake at 350° for 50-60 minutes. Turn upside down on plate; cut and serve while warm.

Carmel-Date Pudding

2 c. all-purpose flour	1 tsp. vanilla
1 c. gran. sugar	½ tsp. almond extract
1½ Tb. baking powder	3½ c. hot water
½ tsp. salt	1 c. packed brown sugar
1 c. DH date nuggets	¼ c. butter or margarine
¼ c. dry milk + ¾ c. water	

Sift flour, sugar, baking powder, and salt together and stir in dates. Stir in milk, vanilla, and almond extract, and mix to stiff batter consistency. Spread in thin layer over bottom of deep 9 x 13 inch baking pan. Combine hot water, butter, and brown sugar, then pour over batter. Bake at 350° for 40-45 minutes. Serve hot or cold.

Low Calorie Whipped Topping

½ c. powdered milk	2 Tb. lemon juice
½ c. ice water	Sugar and vanilla to taste

Mix milk and water at high speed until stiff. Add lemon juice, sugar, and vanilla. Whip until fluffy.

CHAPTER XIII

RECIPES: CAKES

Applesauce or Date Cake

½ c. DH apple or date nuggets
1 c. water
2 tsp. gran. sugar
¼ c. shortening
2/3 c. gran. sugar
½ tsp. vanilla
2 Tb. egg solids + 2½ Tb.
water, (to equal 1 egg)

1¼ c. sifted flour
¼ tsp. cinnamon
¼ tsp. cloves
1 tsp. baking powder
¼ tsp. soda
½ tsp. salt
½ c. raisins

Simmer fruit and water 10 minutes in covered sauce pan, then add 2 tsp. sugar. Cool. Cream shortening, sugar, and vanilla thoroughly. Mix egg into warm water and blend well with fork. Beat in egg until mixture is light. Sift dry ingredients together and add alternately with cooled fruit. Mix until smooth. Stir in raisins until well distributed. Pour into pan and bake about 30 minutes at 350°. Serve with lemon sauce or orange-flavored icing. One 8-inch cake.

Fruited Spice Cake

½ c. DH fruit galaxy
¾ c. water
½ c. shortening
1 c. gran. sugar
¼ c. egg solids + ¼ c. & 1 Tb.
water, (to equal 2 eggs)
2 c. all-purpose flour
2 tsp. baking powder

¼ tsp. salt
1 tsp. cinnamon
½ tsp. ground cloves
½ tsp. nutmeg
¼ c. dry milk + ¾ c. water
¼ tsp. vanilla
½ c. chopped nuts
(optional)

Stir fruit galaxy into water, then bring to a boil and turn off heat. Allow to cool, then drain. Cream shortening and sugar together thoroughly. Add egg solids to dry ingredients. Add sifted dry ingredients alternately with milk. Stir in nuts, vanilla, and drained fruit. Pour batter into oiled loaf pan. Bake at 350° approximately 50-55 minutes. 6 servings.

Fruit Upside Down Cake

¾ c. apricots, fruit galaxy, Peaches, DH
¾ c. boiling water
1/3 c. butter
½ c. packed brown sugar
3 Tb. corn syrup
1 c. sifted all-purpose flour
¼ tsp. salt
¼ c. shortening

½ c. gran. sugar
¼ tsp. almond extract or vanilla
¼ c. egg solids + ¼ c. & 1 Tb. water (to equal 2 eggs)
1½ tsp. baking powder
2½ Tb. dry milk + ¼ c. water

Arrange fruit in bottom of pan, pour in boiling water. Melt brown sugar and butter together until mixture bubbles, add corn syrup and remove from heat. Pour over fruit.

Cake: Mix egg solids with warm water, blend well with fork. Mix milk with warm water and blend well with fork. Cream shortening and sugar together thoroughly. Add almond extract. Beat in eggs, mix well. Sift flour, baking powder, and salt together and add alternately with milk. Pour batter over fruit. Bake at 350° for approximately 35-40 minutes. Turn out of pan immediately. One 9-inch cake.

Scripture Cake
(Just for fun)

2 c. Jeremiah 6:20
1 c. Judges 5:25 (last clause)
6 Tb. Jeremiah 17:11
2 Tb. I Samuel 14:25
½ c. Judges 4:19 (last clause)
Pinch of Leviticus 2:13
4½ c. I Kings 4:22 (1st clause)

4 tsp. Amos 4:5
1 c. Samuel 30:12 (2nd clause)
1 c. Nahum 3:12
1 c. Numbers 17:8
II Chronicles 9:9, as desired

Cream Jeremiah and Judges. Add beaten Jeremiah 17:11, Samuel, Judges 4:19. Sift together dry ingredients and add to above mixture. Beat thoroughly and add Samuel, Nahum, and Numbers. Bake at 350° for 45 minutes or until done when tested with toothpick.

CHAPTER XIV

RECIPES: COOKIES

Apple Cookies

½ c. shortening
2/3 c. sugar
1¾ c. flour
½ tsp. soda
½ tsp. salt
¼ tsp. cinnamon

2 Tb. dry milk + ¼ c. water
2 Tb. dry egg + 2½ Tb.
water
¼ tsp. vanilla
2/3 c. DH apple nuggets

Cream shortening and sugar together thoroughly. Sift flour, soda, salt, and cinnamon together and add to creamed mixture until well blended. Reconstitute milk and eggs together. Blend until smooth. Stir in beaten egg, milk, and vanilla, mixing well. Stir in apple nuggets until blended. Drop by teaspoonfuls on greased cookie sheet. Bake at 400° for 10 minutes. About 3 dozen.

Apple-Oatmeal Cookies

½ c. oil (or shortening)
2/3 c. sugar
1 1/3 c. flour
½ tsp. soda
½ tsp. salt
¼ tsp. cinnamon
1 Tb. dry milk + ¼ c. water

2 Tb. dry eggs + 2½ Tb.
water (to equal 1 egg)
¼ tsp. vanilla
2/3 c. DH apple nuggets
1 c. oatmeal
2/3 c. raisins

Cream shortening and sugar together thoroughly. Sift flour, soda, salt, and cinnamon together, and add to creamed mixture until well blended. Reconstitute milk and egg together. Blend until smooth. Stir in beaten egg, milk, and vanilla, mixing well. Stir in apple nuggets until blended. Add oats and raisins, mixing well. Drop by teaspoonfuls on greased cookie sheet. Bake at 375° for not quite 10 minutes.
 **Variation: Substitute ½ the sugar with honey, and add ½ c. more oats. About 3 dozen.

Chocolate Chip "Oaty" Cookies

¼ c. dry egg + ¼ c. &   1 tsp. baking soda
  1 Tb. water   1 tsp. salt
1 c. shortening   1 tsp. water
¾ c. white sugar   1 tsp. vanilla
¾ c. brown sugar   1 c. quick oats
1 c. sifted whole wheat flour   1 pkg. chocolate chips
1 c. white flour

Reconstitute and blend eggs. Cream sugars, shortening, and eggs until well blended. Add flours gradually. Dissolve baking soda and salt in water. Add to other ingredients. Add vanilla, oats, and chocolate chips. Drop by teaspoonfuls on ungreased baking sheet. Bake at 375° for 10-12 minutes. About 3 dozen.

Date Pinwheels

1 c. DH date nuggets   ½ tsp. vanilla
½ c. water   2 c. flour
¾ c. butter or shortening   ½ c. MPF (or whole wheat
½ c. brown sugar   or white flour)
½ c. white sugar   ½ tsp. soda
¼ c. dry egg + ¼ c. & 1 Tb.   ¼ tsp. salt
  water, beaten (to equal
  2 eggs)

Cook dates in water for five minutes, stirring constantly. Cool. Cream shortening and sugars. Add eggs and vanilla, beat until light and fluffy. Add sifted dry ingredients. Chill dough for half an hour. Pat half of the dough mixture in rectangle on wax paper. Roll carefully to 10 x 14 inches, 1/8 inch thick. Spread half of date mixture onto dough and roll like jelly roll. Wrap in waxed paper. Repeat with remaining dough and chill until firm. Cut into thinly sliced pinwheels. Place on greased baking sheet. Bake at 400° for 7 minutes. About 5½ dozen.

Filled Bar Cookies

Crust:

¾ c. soft shortening, part butter   ½ tsp. soda
1 c. brown sugar   1 tsp. salt
1¾ c. sifted flour   1½ c. quick oats

Mix together thoroughly the shortening and sugar. Sift together and stir in the flour, soda, and salt. Stir in the oats. Mix thoroughly. Place one half of the crumb mixture into a greased and floured 9 x 13 in. pan. Press and flatten with hands to cover bottom of pan. Spread with cooled filling. Cover with remaining crumb mix, patting lightly. Bake until lightly browned. While warm cut into bars and remove from pan. Bake at 400° for 25-30 minutes. 2½ dozen.

Date Filling

2½ c. DH dates
1 c. water

Bring water to a boil; add dates. Cover and remove from heat. Let stand until cooled. The dates do not need any sweetener. When cool spread on first layer of crust.

Date-Apricot Filling

¾ c. DH dates   ½ c. water
1/3 c. water   2 Tb. apricot juice
1 c. DH apricots

Bring water to a boil and add dry fruits. Cook for about ½ hour. Add apricot juice and continue cooking until thickened, about 10 minutes. When cool, spread on first layer of crust.

Prune-Orange Filling

2½ c. DH prunes   2 Tb. lemon juice
½ c. sugar   1 c. water
½ c. orange juice

Bring water to a boil; add prunes and sugar. Cook for ½ hour. Add other ingredients and continue cooking until thickened, about 10 minutes. When cool, spread on first layer of crust.

Galaxy Shortbread

2/3 c. DH fruit galaxy
2 c. water
½ c. butter
¼ c. sugar
1 c. flour + 6 Tb.
½ tsp. baking powder
¼ tsp. salt

1 c. brown sugar, packed
¼ c. dry egg + ¼ c. &
 1 Tb. water, beaten (to
 equal 2 eggs)
½ tsp. vanilla
½ c. nuts, chopped

Put fruit galaxy in water and bring to a boil. Simmer 5 minutes. Allow to cool. Mix butter, sugar, and 1 c. flour until crumbly. Pack into pan. Sift 6 Tb. flour, baking powder, and salt together. Gradually beat brown sugar into eggs; stir into mixture. Add vanilla, chopped nuts, and drained fruit. Spread over packed layer and bake 45 minutes at 325°. Cool in pan. Cut into 1 x 2 inch bars and sprinkle with confectioners sugar. About 32 servings.

Peanut Butter Cookies

½ c. shortening
1 c. raw or brown sugar
2 Tb. dry egg + 2½ Tb. water,
 beaten (to equal 1 egg)
½ c. peanut butter

2 Tb. cream
1 tsp. soda
1½ c. sifted whole wheat
 flour

Cream sugar and shortening. Add egg and peanut butter. Add cream and sifted dry ingredients. Form in balls size of a marble and place on greased cookie sheet. Press both ways with fork dipped in sugar. Bake about 8 minutes at 350°.

Snickerdoodle Cookies

1 c. margarine
1½ c. raw or brown sugar
1 tsp. vanilla
¼ c. dry eggs + ¼ c. &
 1 Tb. water, beaten (to
 equal 2 eggs)
2½ c. sifted whole wheat flour

2 tsp. baking powder
1 tsp. cream of tartar
¼ tsp. salt
¼ c. gran. sugar
2 tsp. cinnamon

Cream margarine and sugar; add vanilla, and beaten eggs.

Sift flour, baking powder, cream of tartar, and salt together twice, and add to creamed mixture. Mix well and chill.

Mix sugar and cinnamon in paper bag. Form dough into balls the size of a large marble, and drop in sugar and cinnamon mixture. Shake to coat. Place on greased cookie sheet 2 inches apart. Bake at 400° for 8-10 minutes.

CHAPTER XV

RECIPES: CEREALS

Corn Meal Mush

1 c. corn meal	3 c. boiling water
1 c. cold water	1½ tsp. salt

Mix corn meal with cold water. Add to salted boiling water. Cover and boil for 30 minutes, stirring occasionally. Serve hot with milk and sugar or honey. (Or add butter, salt, and pepper.)

For fried mush: Pour cereal into a loaf to set. To fry, slice loaf into ½ inch slices. Pan fry in shortening, a few minutes on each side, until it browns. Serve hot with butter or honey, syrup or jam. 5-6 servings.

MPF Porridge

½ c. MPF
1 c. hot or boiling water
2 Tb. honey (optional)

Melt honey in boiling water. Pour over MPF and stir. Add sugar (if honey is not used) and milk to taste.

If you happen to be out of milk, mix ¼ c. dry milk with the MPF and then pour hot water over it.

Wheaty Oatmeal

Prepare your oatmeal as you normally would and stir in ¼-½ c. whole or cracked cooked wheat.

Cracked Wheat Cereal

1 c. cracked wheat	1 tsp. salt
3 c. water	

Pour wheat into salted, boiling water. Boil 15-20 minutes to desired consistency. About 5 servings.

Whole Wheat Cereal
(Cook the night before)

1 c. whole wheat
4 c. water
1 tsp. salt

The night before, add wheat to salted, boiling water. Boil for about 10 minutes, cover and let stand on pilot light overnight. Wheat can be ready to eat by morning. Serve with *warm* milk, sugar or honey, and butter. About 5 servings.

Whole Wheat Cereal
(Cook in a thermos)

Fill thermos ¼ full of wheat. Then fill ¾ full with boiling water. Cap and let stand overnight.

**IDEA: Next time you have whole or cracked wheat for breakfast, put 1 Tb. honey in the water as it cooks.

Had any cooked rice and milk and sugar for breakfast lately? It's really a treat around the house if you will slice a banana in it.

CHAPTER XVI

RECIPES: BREADS, ROLLS, & BISCUITS

No Yeast Whole Wheat Bread

1/3 c. brown sugar
3 Tb. molasses or honey
1 tsp. soda
2 Tb. day egg + 2½ Tb. water,
  (to equal 1 egg)
2 c. whole wheat flour

1 tsp. salt
1½ tsp. butter, melted
2 c. buttermilk
½ c. raisins
½ c. nuts
1 tsp. baking powder

Mix egg, sugar, molasses or honey, and soda. Add gradually sifted whole wheat flour and salt. Mix in remaining ingredients thoroughly. Place in a loaf pan and bake for about 1 hour at 375°. 1 loaf.

Whole Wheat Bread*

1½ c. water
1 can condensed milk
2 Tb. yeast
½ c. water
3 Tb. honey

3 Tb. molasses
4 Tb. liquid shortening
1½ Tb. salt
4 c. whole wheat flour
4 c. white flour

Warm milk and water. Set aside to cool. Dissolve yeast in ½ c. water.

Add honey, molasses, liquid shortening, and salt to cooled milk mixture. Add pre-dissolved yeast. Stir. Add whole wheat flour and beat until smooth. Let stand 5-10 minutes, then add white flour. Knead in more flour if necessary.

Knead and return to greased pan, cover with a warm, dampened cloth. Set in warm place until double. Punch down, cover, and let rise again until double.

Divide into 3 loaves. Place each in a well-greased loaf pan, cover and let rise again. Bake at 350° for about 50 minutes. Remove from pans and place on wire rack to cool. If soft crust is desired, brush with cream or soft margarine. 3 loaves.

Wheat Bread

1½ Tb. dry yeast	3 tsp. salt
1½ c. lukewarm water	3 Tb. brown sugar
2 c. hot water	6 Tb. shortening
¾ c. dry milk	7-8 c. whole wheat flour

Dissolve yeast in 1½ c. lukewarm water, with a little sugar added. Place hot water in a large bowl or pan. Add dry milk, salt brown sugar, and shortening. Mix with electric mixer or hand beater. Gradually add 1 - 2 c. flour and mix. Add yeast and blend. Now slowly and a little at a time add flour, until you can no longer mix with mixer. Then fold in remaining flour, mixing well, until a soft dough is formed. Knead well, shape into a ball, cover and allow to rise until double in size. Punch down gently and shape into loaves, allow to rise for about 20 minutes. Bake at 325° for 1 hour. Remove from oven and take out of pans. Brush with shortening for a soft crust.

White Bread

1½ Tb. yeast	2/3 c. dry milk
3 c. lukewarm water	2 Tb. shortening,
5 c. hot water	heaping
7 tsp. sugar	1½ c. potato flakes
2 tsp. salt	12-14 c. flour

Dissolve yeast in lukewarm water (add ½ tsp. sugar to water). Place hot water in a large bowl or pan. Add sugar, salt, dry milk, shortening, potato flakes and dissolved yeast. Mix well (electric mixer or hand beater can be used). Gradually add flour. Continue mixing until dough gets too stiff for beater. Fold in remaining flour to form a soft dough. Knead very well. Cover and allow to double in size. Punch down, gently, shape in loaves, place in greased pans and allow to rise again. Bake 1 hour at 325°. (This tends to be a sticky dough, but makes a very light, good bread.)

Apricot Bread

1 c. DH apricots (cover	½ c. orange juice
with water	2 c. sifted flour

1 c. sugar
2 Tb. soft butter
2 Ts. dry egg + 2½ Tb. water
  (to equal 1 egg)
¼ c. water

2 tsp. baking powder
¼ tsp. soda
1 tsp. salt
½ c. chopped nuts

Soak apricots in water for 30 minutes. Drain and cut each into 8 pieces with scissors.

Cream sugar, butter, and egg together. Stir in water and orange juice.

Sift flour, baking powder, soda, and salt together. Stir into batter. Blend nuts and apricots and add to batter.

Pour into 1 large or 2 small loaf pans or 3 no. 2 cans (for round shape). Let stand for 20 minutes. Bake loaves 55-60 minutes in 350° oven, or bake small cans for 45-50 minutes. 1 large loaf or 2 small loaves.

Corn Bread or Muffins

1 c. corn meal (yellow) or
  ¾ c. corn meal + ¼ c. MPF
1 c. flour
3½ tsp. baking powder
2 Tb. sugar

1 tsp. salt
2 Tb. egg solids + 2½ Tb.
  water, (to equal 1 egg)
3 Tb. dry milk + 1 c.
  water

Combine dry ingredients including egg and milk. Blend very well until you can see yellow corn meal is even throughout mixture. Add liquid, stir until moist. Batter will be lumpy. Pour into greased 8 x 8 inch pan. Bake at 425° for 25-30 minutes.

For muffins, pour into cupcake papers or muffin tin and bake at 425° for 20 minutes. 8 x 8 inch loaf or 12 muffins.

Date-Nut Bread*

2 c. boiling water
1 tsp. soda
2 c. DH dates
2 Tb. butter or margarine
¼ c. dry egg + ¼ c. & 1 Tb.
  water, (to equal 2 eggs)
2 c. raw sugar

4 c. sifted whole
  wheat flour
½ tsp. salt
2 tsp cinnamon
3 tsp. baking powder
1 c. chopped nuts
2 tsp. vanilla

Combine boiling water and soda, then add dates and butter. Combine beaten eggs and sugar, and add to first mixture. Add flour, salt, spice, and baking powder which have been sifted together twice. Add nuts and vanilla. Pour into loaf pans and let stand for 5 minutes. Bake 1 hour and 15 minutes at 325 - 350°. Loaf pans should be greased and the bottom lined with waxed paper.

This bread is better if baked the day before it is used. Each loaf will yield 20-22 slices. 2 loaves.

Date-Nut Bread

2 c. boiling water	¼ c. dry egg + ¼ c. & 1 Tb.
1½ c. DH dates	water (to equal 2 eggs)
2 tsp. soda	4 c. flour
2 Tb. shortening	1 tsp. salt
1 c. sugar	1 c. nuts, chopped
	2 tsp. vanilla

Pour boiling water over dates, add soda and allow to cool. Cream shortening and sugar, add eggs and mix well. Add flour and salt, vanilla and nuts. Stir until well blended. Pour into greased bread pan. Bake at 325° for 1 hour, or pour into 3 round juice cans, fill 2/3 full. Bake at 325° for 45 minutes.

For Banana Nut Bread: Reconstitute 1 c. DH banana flakes with 1 c. water—add in place of dates to batter and blend well.

Peach or Apricot Nut Bread

½ c. DH peaches or apricots	2 Tb. egg solids + 2½ Tb.
½ c. water	water, (1 egg)
3 c. sifted flour	¾ c. dry milk + 1¼ c. water
1 c. gran. sugar	1 Tb. melted shortening
1 1/3 Tb. baking powder	1 c. chopped walnuts
½ tsp. salt	

Rinse fruit. Put into water and bring to a boil. Remove from heat. Cool, drain, and chop. Sift flour, sugar, baking powder, and salt together. Add egg solids and dry milk to dry ingredients. Combine water and shortening. Stir into flour mixture, blending only until flour is moistened. Stir in chopped fruit and nuts. Turn into greased pan and bake at 350° for 50-60 minutes. Turn out on wire rack to cool. 1 loaf.

Pumpkin Bread

3 c. flour   2 c. sugar
1 tsp. soda   1 tsp. salt
3 tsp. cinnamon   ½ c. nuts, chopped

Mix above ingredients well and add:

1½ c. oil or melted shortening   ½ c. dry egg + 2/3 c.
2 c. pumpkin (one no. 303 can)   water (to equal 4 eggs)

Fold together until just wet. Pour into two greased bread pans. Bake for 1 hour at 350°.

Quick & Easy Nut Bread

¾ c. sugar   ¼ c. chopped nuts
2 Tb. whole egg solids + 2½   3 c. biscuit mix
   Tb. water (to equal 1 egg)   1 c. DH date nuggets (for
½ c. powdered milk   variety use DH apple
1¼ c. water   nuggets)

Mix very well and hard for about 1 minute. Pour into a greased pan. Bake at 350° for 45-50 minutes. 1 loaf.

Spoon Bread*

1 pkg. dry yeast dissolved   1½ tsp. salt
   in 1/3 c. water   2 Tb. whole egg solids +
½ c. dry milk + 1¾ c. warm   2½ Tb. water, beaten
   water   (to equal 1 egg)
1 Tb. oil   3—3½ c. unsifted whole
1-2 Tb. honey or raw sugar   wheat flour

To warm milk add dissolved yeast, egg, oil, honey, and salt. Stir and add flour gradually. Beat vigorously after each addition. Let rise at room temperature for 30 minutes. Stir down and spoon into greased loaf pan. Let rise 30 minutes or until not quite double in bulk. Bake 1 hour at 325 - 350°. 1 loaf.

Spoon Corn Bread

4 Tb. dry milk + 1 c. cold
  water
¼ c. egg solids + ¼ c. &
  1 Tb. water
1 c. corn meal
	1½ tsp. salt
	¼ c. dry milk +
	  2 c. hot water
	3 Tb. melted shortening

Reconstitute eggs and milk in separate bowls. Mix salt and corn meal. Combine with cold milk, stirring until smooth. Add to *hot* milk. Cook, until thickened for about 5 minutes, stirring constantly. Beat eggs. Add eggs and shortening to other ingredients and blend well. Pour into greased 1½ qt. casserole dish. Bake at 350° for 45-50 minutes. Serve hot and top with melted butter and jam of your choice. 1½ qt. casserole.

MPF Biscuits

1½ c. flour ¼ c. MPF 3 tsp. baking powder	1 tsp. salt ¼ c. shortening ¼ c. dry milk + ¾ c. water

Mix dry ingredients. Cut in shortening finely. Stir in water. Round on lightly floured board. Knead lightly (30 seconds). Roll or pat out to ½ inch thick. Cut (use a drinking glass if you have no cutter.) Place on a greased baking sheet and bake 10-12 minutes at 450°. 15-20 biscuits.

Homemade Biscuit Mix

8 c. flour 3 Tb. baking powder 1 Tb. salt	1½ c. shortening ½ c. powdered milk

Cut ingredients together thoroughly. Place in an airtight container for future use. This can be used in any recipe calling for biscuit mix. About 9 cups.

Corn-MPF Griddle Cakes

2 Tb. MPF
2/3 c. corn meal
½ tsp. salt
1/3 tsp. soda
1 tsp. melted fat

½ c. dry milk + ¾ c. water
(recon. and add 1 tsp.
lemon juice or vinegar
to sour)
2 Tb. egg solids + 2½ Tb.
water, beaten (to equal
1 egg)

Add MPF to 1/3 c. milk or water and soak for 15 minutes. Sift the dry ingredients together and add the sour milk, egg, fat, and MPF mixture. Combine and drop by spoonfuls on hot griddle.

Neat-Wheat Coffee Cake

1 c. sugar
½ c. shortening
¼ c. dry egg + ¼ c. & 1 Tb.
water, (to equal 2 eggs)
1 1/8 c. buttermilk

½ tsp. salt
4 tsp. baking powder
1 tsp. soda
1½ c. whole wheat flour
1 tsp. vanilla

Cream shortening and sugar together thoroughly. Add eggs, beat well. Combine all dry ingredients and add alternately with buttermilk. Add vanilla. Mix very well together until mix looks like consistency of white cake. This recipe requires that the ingredients be mixed more thoroughly than when mixing a cake with white flour.

Pour into well-greased and floured 9 x 13 in. cake pan. Sprinkle with topping recipe following. Bake at 350° for 35-40 minutes.

Topping for Neat-Wheat Coffee Cake

¼ c. brown sugar
1 tsp. cinnamon
1 Tb. white flour

1 Tb. melted butter
½ c. chopped nuts

Combine all ingredients and sprinkle on top of cake before baking.

Apple or Date Muffins

1¾ c. sifted all-purpose flour
½ c. packed brown sugar
2½ tsp. baking powder
¾ tsp. salt
¾ tsp. cinnamon

1/3 c. melted shortening
2 Tb. egg solids + 2½ Tb.
   water, (to equal 1 egg)
¼ c. dry milk + ¾ c. water
2/3 c. apple or date
   nuggets, DH

Sift flour, sugar, baking powder, salt, and cinnamon together. Add dry milk and egg solids to dry ingredients. Add water to melted shortening. Make a well in the dry ingredients. Add liquid and stir just until dry ingredients are dampened. Fold in dry fruit nuggets. Fill greased muffin tins 2/3 full and bake at 400° for approximately 20 minutes. 12 muffins.

Potato Doughnuts

2 yeast cakes
10 Tb. (5/8 c.) dry milk +
   3¾ c. water
7/8 c. sugar
1 c. mashed potatoes (add
   ¾ c. instant potato flakes
   to 1 c. hot water and stir)

¾ c. shortening
¼ c. & 2 Tb. dry egg solids +
   ½ c. water, well beaten
   (to equal 3 eggs)
1 Tb. salt
10 c. flour

Dissolve yeast in ½ c. warm water. Scald milk and let it cool. Sprinkle sugar over mashed potatoes. Add shortening and cream well. Add beaten eggs, salt, milk, yeast, and flour in order. Let rise once; punch down. Let rise 1 hour; pat or roll out quite thin. Let rise 10 minutes; cut. Deep fry at 400° until golden brown, turning once. Cool and glaze. 8-10 dozen.

Cornmeal Raised Rolls

2 Tb. dry yeast
¼ c. warm water
¼ c. sugar
¼ c. melted shortening
1 c. corn meal
2¼ c. hot water

2 Tb. egg solids +
   2½ Tb. water, beaten
3 Tb. dry milk + 2/3 c. water
6 c. flour (approximately)
2 tsp. salt

Sprinkle yeast into warm water; let dissolve. Add sugar, oil, and corn meal to hot water, then allow to cool. Add yeast, egg, milk, and half of flour, and salt to mixture, mix to a smooth batter. Then add enough flour to form a soft dough. Mix well, let stand about 20 minutes. Form into rolls, let rise until very light. Bake at 375° for 25-30 minutes. 2 dozen rolls.

Potato Rolls

1 Tb. dry yeast
¾ c. dry milk + 1½ c. water
¼ c. sugar
¼ c. shortening
1½ tsp. salt

¼ c. potato flakes
2 Tb. dry egg + 2½ Tb.
    water, beaten (to equal
    1 egg)
2¼ - 3 c. flour

Soften yeast in ¼ c. warm water. Scald milk. Mix milk, salt, sugar, shortening and potato flakes. Cool. Add yeast and beaten eggs. Add 2 c. flour and beat well. Add the rest of the flour to make a soft dough. Let rise, punch down and let rest 10 minutes. Form into rolls. Let rise and bake at 400° 10-12 minutes. 2 dozen rolls.

Easy Popovers

1 c. flour
¼ tsp. salt
¼ c. + 2 Tb. whole egg solids

½ c. water
¼-½ c. dry milk + 1 c. water
1 Tb. melted margarine

Preheat oven to 400°. Grease 6 oven glass custard cups. Mix the dry ingredients well. Combine liquid ingredients, add these to the dry ingredients and beat until smooth. Fill the cups about ¾ full. Bake until well browned, about 50 minutes. When done, prick tops to allow the steam to escape. Serve with butter and jelly, or split and fill with creamed beef, chicken, seafood, etc. 6 popovers.

Waffles

1 c. sifted whole wheat flour
3 tsp. baking powder
½ tsp. salt
2 tsp. sugar

2 eggs, separated
¼ c. oil
¾ c. dry milk +
    1½ c. water

Sift dry ingredients 3 times. Add egg yolks and milk gradually, beating with electric mixer on low speed. Add oil. Batter will be very thin. Beat hard for 2 minutes. Fold in beaten egg whites. Bake in preheated waffle iron.

**Variation: You may add ½ tsp. soda and substitute buttermilk for milk to make a richer waffle.

Homemade Noodles

¼ c. egg solids + ¼ c. &   ¼ tsp. salt
  1 Tb. water, beaten   ¼ tsp. baking powder
  (to equal 2 eggs)   Flour

Add enough flour to make a stiff batter. Roll until very thin and cut with a cutter or knife. Use plenty of flour to roll dough in. After cutting put noodles in left over flour. Drop in broth and cook 5-10 minutes. Small batch.

*These recipes were originally printed in *Wheat For Man* by Vernice Rosenvall, Mabel Miller, and Dora D. Flack. They are used here by permission of the authors.

CHAPTER XVII

RECIPES: YEAST

Sourdough Starter

2 c. flour
1 Tb. dry yeast
2 c. warm water

Combine ingredients and blend very well. Put in warm place, cover with a towel, overnight or all day. When ready to use, put half of start in a covered jar and store in the refrigerator. If it is replenished every week with flour and water, your start can last for months and months.

Sometimes use milk instead of water when you "feed" or replenish your start. Be sure to beat it well and allow to stand overnight to develop. Always remember to take half out and put it away for your future use. The longer it is fed and replaced to develop the more "sour" your dough will become.

Everlasting Yeast

1 qt. warm potato water   2 Tb. sugar
½ Tb. dry yeast   2 Tb. flour
1 level tsp. salt

Mix all of the ingredients well. Place in a warm area to raise, until ready to use to bake with. Keep half the amount for a "start" next time. Feed with the same ingredients for the next baking. Each time remember to keep half and use half. Refrigerate.

Dry Yeast

For measuring: 1 Tb. of dry yeast equals 1 small envelope of yeast or 1 cake of yeast.

A pinch of sugar helps the yeast develop better, when added to warm water.

A can of yeast is good for 1-1½ years if kept in the refrigerator with a plastic lid on the can, provided you haven't stored it too long before opening the can.

**IDEA: Add ½ c. DH apple nuggets or date nuggets to your pancake or muffin dough. Makes a nice change.

CHAPTER XVIII

RECIPES: SOAP

Grandmother's Homemade Soap

1 can lye
19½ c. warm water
12 c. clean grease

¼ c. ammonia
½ c. borax

Dissolve lye in water. Let cool until lukewarm. Melt grease. Cool to lukewarm. Add to lye. Add ammonia and borax. Stir until thick. Pour into containers. Let set a few days then cut into squares.

Homemade Soap*

3 cans Lewis lye
10 qts. water
12 lbs. crackling or lard
18 qts. water

Mix lye and 10 qts. water, bring to a boil. Add 12 lbs. cracklings or lard and boil slowly for 1 hour. Then add 18 qts. water and continue cooking. When mixture is consistency of heavy syrup pour into a mold. Cut into bars when cold.

Laundry Soap

1 can lye
½ c. borax
5 lbs. grease

½ c. ammonia
½ c. kerosene

---

*This recipe was given to me by a little old lady in an antique shop. She told how many times her pioneer grandmother had used it when they made their own soap and candles.

Melt lye in quart of water. Dissolve the borax in 1 cup water and add to lye mixture. Melt grease and add ammonia and kerosene. Add to lye. Stir until it thickens. Pour into molds, or use milk cartons. (You could use a grater to make a powdered-type soap.)

Tips to follow when making soap:

Always use a heavy metal container when making soap!

Be aware of what you're working with. Keep all lyes, kerosene, and ammonias away from children!

It has been suggested that when you work with lye it should be outside, if possible. The odors and fumes from it are very strong.

Molds can be made out of wood, like a trough, to pour soap into.

CHAPTER XIX

SUGGESTED SOURCES FOR FURTHER INFORMATION

The ABC's of Home Food Dehydration, Barbara Densley, Horizon Publishers and Distributors, P.O. Box 490, Bountiful, Utah 84010.

Adventures in Cooking (wheat germ), Krestmer Wheat Germ Co.

Ball Blue Book, Home Canning Manual, Dept. PK-6, Box 2005, Muncie, Indiana.

Basic Home Storage Guide, Randall K. Mehew, Horizon Publishers and Distributors, P.O. Box 490, Bountiful, Utah 84010.

Bee Prepared with Honey, Arthur W. Andersen, Horizon Publishers and Distributors, P.O. Box 490, Bountiful, Utah 84010.

Beginner's Guide to Family Preparedness, Rosalie Mason, Horizon Publishers and Distributors, P.O. Box 490, Bountiful, Utah 84010.

Boy Scout Field Book, Boy Scouts of America, New Brunswick, New Jersey.

Boy Scout Handbook, Boy Scouts of America, New Brunswick, New Jersey.

Creative Wheat Cookery, Evelyn C. Ethington, Horizon Publishers and Distributors, P.O. Box 490, Bountiful, Utah 84010.

Family Storage Plan, Bob Zabriskie, Bookcraft, Inc., Salt Lake City, Utah.

Fun with Fruit Preservation, Dora D. Flack, Horizon Publishers and Distributors, P.O. Box 490, Bountiful, Utah 84010.

Gateway to Survival, Walter D. Batchelor, Bookcraft, Inc., Salt Lake City, Utah.

Home Food Dehydrating, Jay & Shirley Bills, Horizon Publishers and Distributors, P.O. Box 490, Bountiful, Utah 84010.

Home Freezing of Fruits and Vegetables, Home Garden Bulletin 10, U.S. Dept. of Agriculture.

Honey, Some Ways to Use It, Home Garden Bulletin 37, U.S. Dept. of Agriculture.

Home Garden Hints, Alan K. Briscoe, Horizon Publishers and Distributors, P.O. Box 490, Bountiful, Utah 84010.

The Improvement Era, 1956 issues, LDS Church
This year's issues of the *Era* ran a series of articles on the storage programs, with one article appearing each month. They contain pertinent information such as plans for shelves, basics to store, how to care for foods, etc.

Kerr Home Canning Book, Dept. 127, Sand Springs, Oklahoma 74063.

Natural Foods Storage Bible, Sharon Dienstbier and Sybil Hendricks, Horizon Publishers and Distributors, P.O. Box 490, Bountiful, Utah 84010.

Passport to Survival, Esther Dickey, Bookcraft, Inc., Salt Lake City, Utah.

Project: Readiness, Louise E. Nelson, Horizon Publishers and Distributors, P.O. Box 490, Bountiful, Utah 84010.

Soybean Granule Recipes, Alan K. Briscoe, Horizon Publishers and Distributors, P.O. Box 490, Bountiful, Utah 84010.

Sprouting for All Seasons, Bertha B. Larimore, Horizon Publishers and Distributors, P.O. Box 490, Bountiful, Utah 84010.

Tasty Imitations, Barbara G. Salsbury, Horizon Publishers and Distributors, P.O. Box 490, Bountiful, Utah 84010.

Timely Tips on Quantity Food Buying, Alan K. Briscoe, Horizon Publishers and Distributors, P.O. Box 490, Bountiful, Utah 84010.

Wheat for Man, Rosenvall, Miller, Flack, Bookcraft, Inc., Salt Lake City, Utah.

Wheat Germ Recipes, Fisher Wheat Germ, Fisher Flouring Mills, Seattle, Washington.

Your Guide to Home Storage, Alan K. Briscoe, Horizon Publishers and Distributors, P.O. Box 490, Bountiful, Utah 84010.